Christine Watkins's  ion of conversion
stories prompted by her proof of the
good fruits of this or are direct, honest, heart-rending, an — racuious.

Wayne Weible
Author of *Medjugorje: The Message*

Twenty-four years ago Cardinal Hans Urs von Balthasar warned:
"There is only one danger alone for Medjugorje—that people will pass
it by." Christine Watkins's book helps ensure that won't happen. Start
reading and you'll find it hard to put down! These same graces await
us all.

Denis Nolan
Author of *Medjugorje and the Church*

In compelling fashion, Christine Watkins shares her own and five
other first-person accounts of healing and conversion through the
remarkable intercession of our Blessed Mother. The voices shared in
Full of Grace will draw you closer to Jesus Christ through his mother
Mary.

Lisa M. Hendey
Author of *The Handbook for Catholic Moms*

In the true-life stories of Christine Watkins's book, a common refer-
ence point is how extremely lost each person was and how great was
the mercy of God and the tender love of Our Lady interceding for each
of them that brought them to the faith. Their lives could be called stories of "extreme conversion," yet readers will find that this book is as
much about themselves as it is about the writers.

Bernard J. Bush, S.J.
Author of *Living in His Love*

How much do those caught in the coils of life's deceptive attractions
long to think there is a way out? I praise God that the subjects of these
conversion stories care enough about us to bare their souls so that
others might have hope. Who could resist the arms outstretched of
Jesus and Mary as depicted by these desperate souls? Read this book.
Rejoice. Give it to everyone you know who is looking for happiness in
the wrong places and is desperate for salvation.

Ronda Chervin
Author of *Help in Time of Need*

Grace-filled moments are life changing. In this inspiring book of life stories, Christine tenderly touches the depths of people's raw experiences and communicates God's loving truth, igniting this hope: "If God can do it for them, he can do it for me."

Linda Schubert
Author of *Miracle Hour*

I highly recommend reading this book to experience and reflect on our own lives and [to discover] how our stories meld together. In addition, the thought-provoking questions of faith can help draw us to a deeper relationship with Mary our spiritual Mother, and with God. A must-read book to experience Mary's love in our lives.

Fr. Jim Caldwell
Diocese of Tulsa

When heaven draws near to earth lives are profoundly changed. These moving stories of God's intervention will be a legacy of God's love planted in your heart and become a doorway for you to be touched by his mercy.

Neal Lozano
Author of *Unbound: A Practical Guide to Deliverance*

Christine Watkins presents us with deeply inspirational testimonies of six individuals who tangibly experienced Mary's motherly protection and care and her call to give their hearts and minds to her Son through lives of service and intercession. These uplifting accounts and the reflections, scripture passages, and thought-provoking questions that follow are sure to help one grow in faith. This book was a blessing to me. May it be a powerful instrument in God's hands to draw lives to his grace.

Anthony Rosevear, O.P.
Novice Master
Western Dominican Province

I cannot think of another work on Medjugorje so well done! *Full of Grace* certainly caught my attention! While many other works on Medjugorje focus on the facts, figures, historical dates, and messages of the apparitions, they seem far less significant than the personal stories of miraculous conversion that have been captured in this remarkable book. *Full of Grace* is a magnificent blend of real life dramas that reveal the depth of Mary's power to intercede for us. This book will inspire you to call upon her.

Theresa Burke
Founder
Rachel's Vineyard Ministries

FULL
OF
GRACE

Miraculous Stories of Healing
and Conversion through
Mary's Intercession

Christine Watkins

ave maria press A m P notre dame, indiana

Founded in 1865, Ave Maria Press is a ministry of the Indiana Province of Holy Cross.

www.avemariapress.com

ISBN-10 1-59471-226-3   ISBN-13 978-1-59471-226-5

Cover photo of Mary © superstock.com.

Cover and text design by Andy Wagoner.

Printed and bound in the United States of America.

Library of Congress Cataloging-in-Publication Data

Full of grace : miraculous stories of healing and conversion through Mary's intercession / [compiled by] Christine Watkins.

p. cm.

ISBN-13: 978-1-59471-226-5 (pbk.)

ISBN-10: 1-59471-226-3 (pbk.)

1. Mary, Blessed Virgin, Saint--Apparitions and miracles--Bosnia and Hercegovina--Medugorje. 2. Catholics--Biography. 3. Catholic converts--Biography. 4. Spiritual healing--Catholic Church. 5. Religious awakening--Catholic Church. 6. Medugorje (Bosnia and Hercegovina)--Religious life and customs. I. Watkins, Christine.

BT660.M44F86 2010

232.91'7092249742--dc22

[B]

2009049539

This book is dedicated to the best friend I've ever had:
my husband, and my love,

JOHNNY

CONTENTS

FOREWORD

Mary, the Mother of God, in her regular appearances at Medjugorje, comes as a young woman of the local Croatian region of Bosnia and Herzegovina in the former Yugoslavia. She speaks in the local dialect, with the accent of the people who live there. She has always spoken as a loving mother to those who see her—not an archetype, not a mythical personage, but a real person with real reactions and real emotions—with a mother's heart.

Mary began to come to Medjugorje on June 24, 1981, appearing and speaking to a small group of local teenagers. Since then she has come on a regular basis to those same persons, now married men and women, wherever in the world they may be, whether in the United States, in Italy, or in Bosnia and Herzegovina.

The events at Medjugorje are standard for authentic Marian apparitions: all the approved apparitions of Mary have involved certain characteristics that are highly unusual.

Why does the Lord use such strange, even bizarre measures, such as apparitions, to speak to us? He wants us to pay attention. We have ears, but we have not been listening; we have eyes, but we have not been looking. To the deaf, the Lord needs to shout; for the nearly blind, he needs to draw large and startling pictures. God does these things because he loves us, and he wants us to hear what he has to say, to see in faith what he wants us to see.

The theological word for this kind of divine discourse is *apocalyptic*. The word *apocalyptic* describes a revelation that breaks in from the future, somehow entering the present in order to encourage us to turn to God more seriously and to console us by reassuring us that the Lord is Lord of history and of the whole world. The Medjugorje events fit the apocalyptic genre: Mary, already assumed into heaven, into the ultimate future beyond the end of history and the beginning of the world to come, breaks into our present to speak to us, to encourage us, to console us, and to call us to turn more to God.

Medjugorje is not the only series of apparitions having a strong apocalyptic cast; so did the Marian apparitions at Lourdes and at Fatima, and in other places at other times. But Mary's appearances at Medjugorje seem in many ways especially and strongly apocalyptic. All the elements of an apocalyptic event present themselves at Medjugorje: the secrets with their hidden content of troubles to come, the messages' frequent references to the devil, the promise of an eventual permanent sign, the mysterious lights and the behavior of the sun, visions by many people, healings of all kinds, and especially conversions of heart. All of these get our attention, and they proclaim the Lord's power to save us from evil.

There is more to contemporary Marian apparitions than the fact that some of the faithful piously believe in them: contemporary Marian apparitions are much more than objects of pious belief. Through these apparitions God is speaking; God is acting.

Through the facts and the circumstances of the appearances of the Mother of God, as well as through her messages, God speaks to us. He admonishes us. He calls us to repentance. He reassures us that he cares and that he holds the present and the future in his all-powerful and loving hands.

In a particular and moving way, God speaks to us through the stories of the people in *Full of Grace* whose lives have been transformed by Mary and her apparitions at Medjugorje. Their stories, and those of many others who have prayed to Mary because of the events at Medjugorje, can have a powerful impact on us.

These are witness stories. They give testimony to this fact: the Lord speaks, acts, gives great graces, and does marvelous things through Mary and for you and me. These inspiring true stories tell us who God and Mary truly are for each one of us.

Fr. Robert Faricy, S.J.
Emeritus Professor of Spirituality
Pontifical Gregorian University, Rome, Italy
May 2009

ACKNOWLEDGEMENTS

It's not every day that one gets an unmistakable and unexpected call from God. This book is such a call. One sunny afternoon while on pilgrimage in Medjugorje back in 2002, I was relaxing on my bed in the pension where I was staying, talking to my traveling companion. I wondered aloud whether it was my idea or God's spurring me to scribble embarrassing snippets of my life onto torn scratch paper and throw them into a big cardboard box marked "Autobiography."

I wasn't exactly asking a question and I certainly didn't expect an answer. But with a clear message that at once enflamed and convicted my heart, God said, "It's me! It's me! I've been the One asking you to write a book. Remember, you gave your life to me." Shaken, I thought back to how, shortly after my conversion, I had prostrated myself before the altar at the New Camaldolese Monastery in Big Sur, California, and, when no one was looking, told God aloud, "Lord, I give you all of me. You gave me back my life, and now I give it back to you. It is yours. Do with it as you please." Then he spoke again, "Your time is not your own. This book will help save souls."

Although not a doubt has entered my mind about the initial call I received in Medjugorje to write this book, the journey has required much trust, patience, and frequent meandering into the unknown. I often walked alone along this winding and sometimes murky path that follows almost every "yes" to God, so whenever help came my way, I embraced it, like a starving mendicant, with unbridled gratitude. My warm thanks will forever go to those whom God sent as helpful companions and midwives, leaving a trail of trust in my heart.

First, I offer gratitude to my husband, Johnny, who, when I announced at the end of my pilgrimage that I'd received a call from God to write a book, wondered if I had taken off in my first flight from reality. When he realized I wasn't veering from the call—even rearranging my life to accommodate it—and when he discovered he actually liked what I was writing, he declared himself the book's co-conspirator and became my indispensably ruthless editor.

I also must single out my wonderful editor, Elianne Obadia, the original "Writer's Midwife," who became so much more to me than that after she spontaneously offered her services upon seeing some of the stories. "The Holy Mother is asking me to help you," she said. Since that moment, I've considered her my Tinkerbell-in-a-good-mood, who flew in just in time to help me give birth to this book and made the connection with Ave Maria Press that led to its publication.

Hugs to Frances Good, who, just because she's my friend, was willing to read stories over and over.

Special thanks to Thomas Grady, Robert Hamma, Amanda Williams, Mary Andrews, Julie Cinninger, Susana Kelly, and Andy Wagoner at Ave Maria Press. With graciousness, talent, and encouragement, they brought this book out into the world.

A thousand thank-yous to those who have shared their remarkable lives with me, some of which grace the pages of this book, and others that I hope will grace future projects. Your courage is formidable. May blessings return to you every time your story touches a heart.

Mother Mary, to you I give my final shower of gratitude. You carried this book under the shadow of your mantle and brought it to completion through a press that gives honor to your name. Thank you for carrying me as well.

INTRODUCTION

As human beings, we sometimes find ourselves in a place devoid of light, filled with sharp edges and sorrow. As we walk forward in this fearsome inner landscape, an abyss opens up before us, and we are helpless not to tumble into it—unless grace extends its gentle hand to save us. We do not always know how we arrived at such a precarious point; but once there, we know we need healing, meaning, love, peace, hope, and happiness. We know that we are seeking something to fulfill us and take away our angst and our sadness. What we do not always know is that we are seeking God.

The true life stories in this book reveal people who have teetered on the edge, in seemingly hopeless situations, and arrived at the other side of grace. As diverse as they are, these individuals—a homeless drug addict, a lonely youth, a Nobel Peace Prize nominee, a nightclub stripper, a cocaine abuser, and a confused atheist—all possess two vital elements in common: they have discovered hope and healing in a loving God, and they received help in their journeys of faith through the Blessed Virgin Mary's presence and messages in Medjugorje.

Following each story is a message that Mary has given to the world, a message that speaks to the storyteller's life, and perhaps to our own. And for those eager to probe the deeper, reflective waters of discipleship—either alone or within a prayer group—a scripture passage, prayerful reflection questions, and a spiritual exercise at the end of each chapter offer an opportunity to enliven our faith.

These explorations can show us where we are on our spiritual journey, as we peer into the places in our lives where God can touch us more deeply, bringing us healing and wholeness, and molding us into the likeness of his Son.

I have had the privilege of meeting each of the protagonists in this book. They came my way providentially and shared their remarkable tales with me, true in every detail. While on pilgrimage in Medjugorje, I encountered the Nobel Peace Prize nominee, the former stripper, and the former homeless drug addict turned happy family man. I was the confused atheist, brought back to life. The one-time cocaine abuser joined my prayer group and became a friend of mine, and the lonely youth became my husband.

Because I wanted the raw candor and the breadth and depth of each person's journey to remain as accessible and immediate to the reader as they were to me when I first heard them, I transcribed and edited the tellers' own words from our lengthy interviews, shaping them into first-person narrative form. In telling their stories, these ordinary people opened the door to their extraordinary lives—to a view more fantastic than fiction—and showed how God lifted them into his loving arms, often out of a living hell, and raised them up to the heights.

One might ask: Are these people telling the truth? Can God do such things in people's lives, or are miracles and dramatic transformations relegated to the pages of the Bible? These questions only the reader can answer, for they lie in the heart, in the delicate balance between empiricism and faith.

Whatever the answers might be for you, may these stories bring you close to the living God and his beautiful mother as they take you on a journey that reveals a Creator who loves us, even when we're at our worst.

ONE

GORAN

A schizophrenic, homeless drug addict calls out to Mary, beginning an ascent from the streets to the life of a happy, healthy family man.

I woke up again. Who knows how long I'd been unconscious. This time I'd downed a bunch of pills, a bottle of vodka, and a shot of heroin; but trying to kill myself never seemed to work.

Shivering, I crawled across the floor of the derelict, windowless building I'd wandered into and pulled a sheet of plastic over my dying body. I just wanted to rest. Unable to sleep for months, I only traveled in and out of nightmares.

It was the middle of winter. I was thirty years old. I had no one and nothing, not even food. As I lay on the floor, staring at the wall, I felt utterly alone—despised. Perhaps this was just another nightmare . . . but the bitter cold that cut into my bones told me otherwise. I felt dead, but I was still alive.

For the first time since I was a child, I began to cry. I tried to pray but I couldn't remember how. I never really learned, and I hadn't ever really tried. What were the words? Through my tears, and from the depths of my soul, I began to call out to the Mother of God . . .

Terrified and Alone,
I Reminded Myself That I Was a Real Man

That night of dejection spent on the cold concrete floor occurred in my hometown of Split, Croatia, on the Adriatic coast. Years of drug and alcohol abuse had brought me to such a state, but even before I turned to substances, my life had its share of sadness.

Tragedy hit our family household early and left a lingering gloom in its wake. When my sister was four, she fell out the fifth-floor window and landed at my mother's feet—dying a couple of hours later. My brother, when only a year old, contracted meningitis and became a deaf-mute. After that, my mother, always in pajamas and glued to the television, drank herself into a serious depression, and was then diagnosed with leukemia. Father, a sailor, worked away from home on a ship, earning bread for the family. While I, with no strong hand or authority to guide me, began to steal bits of money from my mother's purse.

Every moment, I looked to escape my depressing home life by wandering outside or into fantasies. I wanted to be just like my television and film idols, who taught me that a real man had to go to sports games, wear tattoos, start fights, go to jail, and end up with scars on his face. No one taught me that being good could be the most beautiful thing in the world. My friends persuaded me that good traits and softness were for weaklings and women. When I was eleven years old, they encouraged me to smoke and to drink alcohol. This disgusted me, but I figured that real manhood meant holding a cigarette in one hand and a beer in another. Besides, when I drank, I could do things I would never do otherwise.

One day, I stole a car and escaped with two friends from school. We sped to different towns, piercing through traffic, but the police caught up with us. That night, at age eleven, I slept in jail for the first time. Terrified and alone, I reminded myself that I was a real man who knew everything in life and didn't need anything or anybody.

Every Day, I Grew Worse

It might seem that my constant lies, drinking, and small thefts meant that I didn't love my family. On the contrary, I loved them very much, and so I suffered. I searched for comfort in the streets, since I couldn't bear to stay at home and see my mother drunk and depressed or watch my brother in his debilitating condition.

When I was thirteen, my mother died, and my world collapsed around me. My father remarried eight months later. I hated him for replacing my mother, but I hated my stepmother even more. I didn't know why, because she really did bring light into the house. She was a devout, prayerful woman; but the more she prayed, the more I hated her.

I announced every two or three months that I was going to kill myself, but no one believed me. My family and friends thought I was simply passing through an initial stage of shock.

On the first anniversary of my mother's death, I returned home and asked my father if I could chat with him. I wanted to talk about my feelings—everything that was going on in my heart. He was sitting in front of the television, watching the world soccer championship in Argentina. Not bothering to look up, he barked, "You have nothing to say. Get lost in your room, and study!"

I went to my room, took a pistol that I'd borrowed from a friend, put it to my head, and fired.

In a panic, my father sped me to the emergency room, where doctors attempted to remove the bullet that had lodged in my brain. But doing that was too dangerous, so they left it there. When I woke up after surgery, my father and stepmother, trying to ease my worry, told me that the bullet had been successfully removed.

A short time later, I was in a bar when a fight broke out, and someone hit my head with a beer bottle. When I went to the hospital to get stitches, the doctor told me I had something inside my head. I peered at the x-ray—and there was that bullet.

This gave me the excuse I needed to cause chaos. I stormed home, shoved open the front door, and shouted, "You lied to me!" I was always looking for someone to blame. Everyone else was at fault. I was the only good person.

My father saw that something wasn't right with me. He knew the company I kept, but he thought, "He is still young. He'll get over it. These are his crazy years." But I didn't get over it. Every day, I grew worse.

I Was Immediately Addicted

Tiring of alcohol hangovers, I began to mix over-the-counter pills with my drinks. Then one of my friends who had just tried marijuana announced one day, "Forget about alcohol— we just fight and get beat up when we drink. That's crazy. Man, this new stuff is super. You smoke your fill and laugh the rest of the day." My other friends and I grew curious, but we feared marijuana because we didn't want to be drug addicts, only delinquents.

Our friend explained to us, nicely, that marijuana definitely wasn't a drug, or addictive. Not only that, he said, it cleared your mind, improved your studies and behavior, and gave you a great feeling of freedom. So I lit up my first joint—and liked it.

Around that time, I started to get tattoos, images I couldn't explain, even to myself. They certainly never gave off the manly image I was fighting so hard to maintain. At age fifteen, I had the words "Mommy, I love you" inscribed on my right shoulder. A year later, I had a cross on the crest of a mountain tattooed on my left shoulder. Some years after that, I had two hands in prayer, clasping a rosary, drawn over my heart.

As time passed by, though, my tough exterior began to match my hardened interior. With alcohol, pills, and marijuana in my system, I also moved further away from reality. I was beginning to lose it: forgetting things, cursing uncontrollably, and falling deeper into depression and paranoia. I thought that people wanted to kill me; and to numb my insane fears, I drank. Sometimes I tried to cut down or quit the substances, but I couldn't.

Time passed, and I lost my desire to cut back on anything. One day, a friend came to see me and said, "Man, enough of depression and aggression—I have the real thing. I just tried heroin, and there is nothing better in the world. It's madness. It's perfection."

Needing to escape my mental agony, I allowed someone to shoot me up. As the heroin entered my veins, euphoria flooded me. I felt no shame, no embarrassment. An awakening of something like love expanded inside of me, and I wanted to help everyone—or at least give everyone advice. I was immediately addicted.

The next day, I quickly found money and bought more of the drug; but not knowing how to use the needles, I ended up torturing myself. By the time I found a vein, I had covered myself in blood, from the top of my arms to my knees. After that I simply used more alcohol or marijuana to dull my fear of the needles. And heroin didn't cost much, at least at first.

Over time, I needed larger amounts of heroin to achieve the same high, so I started stealing from my parents' house, where I was living. I took gold, plates, vases, mixers, the coffee pot, and more, and sold them cheaply. In the beginning, fifty kunas [about ten dollars] paid for a day's worth of heroin, but after about three or four months passed, crisis struck. I now needed 100 kunas, then 200, 400, 500 each day. Who can earn that kind of money?

Seeing the Truth Shattered His Heart

Then came more craziness. I started stealing outside my home and breaking into cars. With every crisis, I came home drunk, asking my father for more money. He was beside himself with worry, seeing that I was totally out of my mind. One day, while I was out, he went into my bedroom and began searching for evidence that could explain my behavior, and he came across syringes and the band of rubber I used for making my veins pop out.

My father's world crumbled around him. Seeing the truth shattered his heart. He knew I was in trouble, but this . . . ? In an effort to help, he tried to get close to me, but we were too alike, and when our anger flared, he sometimes beat me to bits. Finally, he realized that while I was on heroin I was insane, and there was no point in beating me.

So he tried to extend some sort of love by approaching me to have a talk. But a thick wall towered between us. "What could you possibly tell me now that would make any difference?" I asked him. "Where were you all those wasted years? Leave me alone."

In desperation, my father sent me to the psychiatric unit of Split hospital. There my friends brought me drugs and alcohol. I was a well-seasoned actor. I had a different story for every doctor and nurse and always got what I wanted. I knew when and how to be lovable. I even knew how to cry to attract pity and attention. The doctors never noticed anything wrong with me. On the contrary, they proclaimed my father insane for bringing me there, since I was the one good boy in the whole ward.

Together We Declined into Decay

When I got out of the hospital, I returned to shooting heroin and spending time with a girlfriend named Zeljka. She was essentially drug-free, but often asked me to give her some heroin to try because she saw that when I was using, I behaved well, slept well, and seemed to be happier. I knew that if I started having to share my heroin, it would cost me more money, so I told her I didn't think it was a good idea. Eventually she said, "Listen, if you don't let me try heroin, I'll go see my other friends, and they'll give it to me."

"Uh-oh," I thought, "if she goes to them, she'll get involved with another man who will supply her." I wanted her to be my marionette, my doll—to spend her time only with me. A few times I even beat her because I heard she was out with other friends. So I decided to give her some of my stash, and together we declined into decay. To support her growing habit, she, too, began to steal from my father's house.

In another attempt to help me, my father found me a job, reasoning that if I worked eight hours a day with his friends, in healthy surroundings, perhaps I would change. He made a huge mistake. I disgraced him. I stole from half of the company, and came to work sporadically and drunk. One day I even raised a knife to my boss, and so they finally threw me out.

Zeljka Got Pregnant

Zeljka and I stayed together for almost six years. I thought I was in love with her. I even had the words "I love you Zeljka" tattooed on my arm. And she believed she was in love with me.

At one point, Zeljka got pregnant. She wanted the baby, but I didn't think our lifestyle could support a child. When she was three months pregnant, Zeljka wanted us to change the way we were living and start on the right road, but I decided that she should abort the baby.

Zeljka borrowed money for the abortion, and together she and I went to a private doctor in Split. She handed me the money to pay the doctor when he was done. What happened next, in truth, reveals what kind of a man I was. While she was lying on the operating table, I ran out of the waiting room and spent the money to get high. And that, in essence, was the end of us.

Even with the little self-esteem she had, Zeljka finally understood that I was no good. When she left me, I was devastated. I had thought I was in love. In truth, she had just been another one of my habits. If I had loved her, I would surely never have treated her as I did. Still, I felt angry and betrayed, and I had "don't" added to my "I love you Zeljka" tattoo.

My Father Saved My Life

I continued in my wayward direction, and one day, coming home drunk and in a crisis, as usual, I asked my father to give me money. But he had had enough. He drew back his fist and hit me in the left eye. Without hesitating, I pulled out a small knife and stabbed him in the left side of his abdomen. The police came, dragged me out of the house, and locked me up.

After a few months, I was released. With nowhere else to go, I went home. I stood outside the front door of my father's house and asked to come in, but this time my father made the smartest move possible—one that saved my life.

He locked the door and told me through the cracks, "My son, you are not welcome in this house because all your life you could have chosen your family over the company of your friends in the streets, but you chose them. You are old enough and smart enough to decide what you want, so you can have your friends. Drug yourself, go out into the streets; and one day, if you decide to come back, we will give you all the help necessary to be normal, to be yourself again." I had hated my father all my life, but in that moment, no words could describe my rage.

They Sent Me to a Psychiatric Ward

For nine years, from age twenty-two to thirty-one, I slept in the streets. For nine years, I detested my father and that family of mine. My hatred brought me to madness, and at the same time, it kept me alive, able to sleep out in the streets, those God-forsaken streets.

During those years, God came into the picture only when I used his name to curse. I often bought and sold drugs around churches and shouted insults at the people going in. And the only time I went inside a church was to steal the money out of the collection box.

At first, I had a few friends who let me sleep in their homes—if I had money or drugs to share—but after I hadn't taken a bath for several months, I smelled like a decaying animal, so everyone started to avoid me. I began sleeping in old wooden sheds, on the sidewalk, in parks, and under bridges. I lived like a sick, rabid dog, left to fend for itself, as I rotated between the streets and jail. My daily routine became breaking into homes and apartments and threatening people at gunpoint. My own brother would walk to the other side of the street to avoid me.

Many times, when I spiraled into a dark depression, nothing could calm me down—not drugs, not booze—nothing. Seeking relief, I sometimes took a knife, a piece of glass, or a razor, and cut my arms, neck, and face. I watched the blood pouring out, and it gave me a strange kind of calmness.

The authorities and social workers in Split had no idea what to do with me. Finally, after twenty-seven house breakins, store robberies, and purse or wallet snatchings, they agreed that I should receive punishment. They sent me to a town outside of Zagreb, the capital of Croatia, to a psychiatric ward with locked doors. I walked through those doors sad and scared, because 90 percent of the residents had killed people and were diagnosed with serious mental illnesses. I received therapy with injections and pills, and I came to see that I was just a plain drug addict who overcame my fear of others by acting aggressively, while the other residents were psychopathological murderers who liked to kill. I decided this wasn't the place for me and started to plan my escape.

First I had to steal some money, then get some clothes other than the pajamas all of us had to wear. The clothes came easily. To get the money, though, I stole from a man who had committed four murders—with an axe. But I didn't care. I was blinded by the hope of a trip out of town.

I managed to escape to Split, where I lived as a fugitive because there was a warrant out for my arrest. For three weeks, I managed not to get caught, but during that time, I contracted hepatitis C and turned completely yellow. When the authorities found me again, they immediately shipped me back to the ward. I felt terrified to return. I knew that the quadruple murderer was aware I had stolen his money, and that he was in the ward for life, so I figured he would kill me sooner or later.

The moment I entered the asylum doors, the doctor put me into a room and beat me almost senseless. At one point, he drove his fist into my stomach and said, "I am God here. I can do what I want. I can kill you if I want to." He and the staff then put me into a straightjacket and tied my legs to a bed.

And then came the worst punishment. With cruel calculation, they placed me in the same room with that murderer. What horror. For seven days, he just sat there and looked at me, calmly, with eyes of ice. Every time he got up, I wet myself from fear. I knew that people were murdered, in that asylum, for much less than what I had done.

On the seventh day, he broke his silence. "Listen, you vermin druggie . . ." and then he cursed my mother. "For seven days, I've been thinking to myself, 'Will I choke you or not?'" Then he said, "You know who I am, what I am, and what I did. And I really did decide to choke you like a rabbit. But then I thought, 'If this guy had the courage to steal money from me, I admire him.'" He then stood up and put a cigarette in my mouth.

From that moment on, he fed me at mealtimes, untied my legs and took me to the toilet, took off my pajamas when I had bowel movement, and even wiped my behind.

Even after my week in hell ended, each day was an ugly, frightening experience. Many of my teeth and most of my hair fell out while I was there. I knew I didn't belong in that place, but what could I do? I had to put up with the punishment, and now, because of my escape, I would be detained another six months. The chief doctor on the ward told me that if I committed one more criminal act when I got out he would see to it that I returned and stayed forever. So, I decided that I would never use drugs again. When my sentence was over, I planned to return to Split, find a job, rent a little room, and somehow begin to live normally.

When my day to leave was finally announced, a fear of the outside world seized me so fiercely that the night before my release, I grabbed a razor and cut my veins. The staff patched me up the next morning and set me free.

I Was Waiting for My Time to Die

I went to Zagreb, about eighty kilometers [fifty miles] away. As soon as I got there, I purchased two containers of pills for schizophrenia, took ten of them, and drank two liters of wine. I felt deathly afraid of returning to that mental institution, yet I had no capacity to be a man good to his own word. In that hour and a half, I had forgotten the past two and a half years of my life.

Shortly after that, I returned to Split, but by then, I had ruined myself completely. I couldn't sleep. I couldn't eat. I am a tall man, and I weighed about 56 kilos [123 pounds]. I felt far too weak to break into houses. I could hardly walk. People spat at me. They beat me, harassed me, cursed me, and chased me from their districts, calling me a lousy, sick pest. I begged the dealers I knew to give me drugs but they refused. In the streets, when you have money, you have friends; when you don't have money, you don't have anyone.

I had long ago grown tired of living and lost all hope of ever getting well. I lived from moment to moment, hour to hour, day to day, just waiting for my time to die.

"Do Something to Change This Poor Life of Mine"

So on that night when I lay huddled and shaking, in that derelict building with only cardboard to lie on and a piece of filthy plastic to cover myself, I was at the end of everything.

Until dawn broke, I stared, as I did every night, at a blank wall. But this night, it was different. I was almost a dead man. I started to look at my past through a different lens. I don't know how, but in one single moment, I was able to see what my abject misery and suffering hadn't been able to show me for years.

I thought of all I had done to my family, all my stealing, my lying, my aggression, my hatred. I realized I hated everyone —old ladies, children, men, women—I hated them all and treated them with contempt because I believed this world no longer had any more good people in it. All who remained were horrible, evil, and rotten.

I thought back to the many times, hundreds of times, that I had almost died from dangerous doses of heroin, alcohol, and pills. I'd even shot myself in the head. "Why am I still alive?" I wondered.

In that moment, my eyes opened, and I saw that I was the problem. I was the only villain, the one to blame for what had happened to me in this wasted life. I felt sorry, truly sorry, for all I had done.

And then I started to cry. I wanted to pray, but I didn't even know how to say an Our Father or a Hail Mary. My family was supposedly Catholic, but we never prayed; we never even talked about prayer. My parents never went to church

13

or mentioned faith, although they insisted that I go to church and receive the Sacraments regularly. But that had been long ago. Unable to remember any traditional prayers, I cried out, "Mother of God, please take me up to yourself. Do something to change this poor life of mine. Extend your arms, I beg you."

"Go to Medjugorje and Ask for Help"

Two or three days after my painful cry to the Mother of God, I stumbled into a park at around 7:30 in the morning and sat down on a cold bench. The frigid air stung my skin, and I felt lost, and small as a mouse. I was unsure where to go, penniless and homeless, with no friends, not even a cigarette. I looked into the distance and saw a woman turning a corner to walk into the park toward me. As she got closer, I grew frightened. I wondered if I should flee, but then I thought, "Maybe she'll just pass by, or perhaps she's not coming toward me, and it's just my paranoia." But she came right up to me and said, "Good morning."

Suspicious, I replied, "Good morning."

She told me she had a problem and asked if I could help. I looked at her and thought, "Run, woman! I have no idea what to do with myself, much less how to resolve anybody else's problems. I cause problems. Leave me alone."

But she held on to me like a leech and said, "No, no . . . please. I am looking for a young man. I heard that he hangs around these quarters. They call him Cuke."

Cuke was my nickname [pronounced "chewkee"]. She was looking for me. Now I didn't know what to do. If I told her I was Cuke, who knew what kind of grievance she might have against me? Perhaps I had broken into her house or sold drugs to her child. I decided I didn't care. So, I said, "It's me, lady."

If she caused me any trouble, I would hit her with my fist and leave.

She started to cry. Staring at her in amazement, I thought, "This woman is crazy, 100 percent crazy. No one cries for me." Then she took me by the arm and told me that we should take a little walk.

Before we moved away, she said, "Please, just take the stuff out of your pockets and throw it away—the band of rubber, the syringes, the spoon." That stuff was everything to me, but I listened to her, and I don't know why, because I had never listened to anybody in my life.

As we walked through the park, she told me that she was the mother of one of my acquaintances. This young man was also a drug addict who had ended up in prison. We weren't friends at all; not even close acquaintances. She often visited her son in prison, and he always found time to tell her about me, which is very strange because drug addicts are usually very selfish. Eventually, he talked his mother into looking for me, saying that I was a good man, deserving of help—that I was alone, abandoned by everyone, and would end up killing myself.

If I'd had any money, I would have escaped from her, but I might not have gotten very far. Now that she'd found me, she was determined to help me in any way she could. Since I had no personal documents of any kind, she ran around for about two weeks to get them. Then she took me to the bus station, bought me a ticket, and gave it to the driver so I wouldn't be able to sell it for drugs. "Goran," she said, with deep pity in her eyes, "go to Medjugorje. Our Lady is appearing there. In Medjugorje, there is a community of young men with the same problems as yours. Go there and ask for help."

Convinced that there was no way back from heroin, I had no interest in a rehabilitation home, nor was I consciously aware that the Mother of God was answering my cry for help and holding out her hands to me. Nevertheless, I couldn't handle any more cold winters and wasted years in the street, so I thought, "Who cares? I'll go. I'll stay there two or three months, and then, in the summer, I'll come back to Split. By then, hopefully, I'll be a little bit healthier and able to sleep. Whatever this place is, they'll probably have a bed for me, something to eat, and at least I won't be alone."

When I arrived in Medjugorje, the winter sun had set early and the streets were dark. I walked into a store to ask the woman behind the counter where I could find the rehabilitation community. When she learned I had arrived from Split and didn't know the local area, she called her husband immediately. Within minutes, he drove up, put me in his car, gave me a box of cigarettes, and drove me to the community, which was called Communitá Cenacolo. As he left me at the gate, he looked me in the eye and said, "Go and be successful! You don't need the life you've lived." I felt so touched by this moment that I will never forget it.

For the First Time, I Had to Face Myself

The guys at Cenacolo and Sister Elvira, the community foundress, took me in immediately, without any preliminaries or interviews, although normally a new person is accepted into the community only after two to three months—and even then, only if they show persistence in their desire to stay.

It wasn't long before I realized that all my hellish years in the street, the craziness I had caused, and the depression I had undergone were minor struggles compared to the problems that faced me in this community. Here, for the first time in my life, I had to face myself—a self I did not know, because I had never been normal . . . not for one hour, not even for one minute. All those years, I didn't know who or what I was. I didn't even know what I looked like.

In the Cenacolo community I started to tell the truth for the first time. Ever since I was little I had always pretended, telling lies because I was afraid people would judge me. But this only postponed the judgment, and when it finally came, the punishment was worse than if I had faced it in the moment. But no one had been able to convince me of that. Here, every time I ruined or broke something, I was required (as were the other guys) to stand up in front of everyone at mealtime and admit my mistake, my carelessness—whatever I had done. The fear of condemnation made me tremble in those moments. But the condemnation never came—only support and encouragement.

And then there was prayer. We prayed three rosaries a day, attended three Masses each week, and sat in adoration of the Blessed Sacrament, alone or in a group. I detested this. I thought I had come to Cenacolo to get over my addiction. What did God and prayers have to do with that? So I refused to pray or kneel. The others told me, "No problem. If you don't want to pray, that's okay. Come to the chapel and just sit. We'll pray for you." All of this seemed very strange. I couldn't believe someone would actually pray for me and not expect anything in return.

Despite all the kindness I was shown, I wanted to leave at least a thousand times. But my desire to go was never as strong as some inner or outer power I didn't know or understand that wanted me to stay to the end.

And so I lived the community's rhythm of life. I had enormous struggles, problems, and paranoia; but my conversion, like most others' there, was, in truth, relatively short because, twenty-four hours a day, the guys were after me to improve and keep moving forward.

I had entered community life afraid of being alone, afraid of being with others, afraid of weakness, afraid of living without drugs, afraid to look in the mirror, afraid to pray. Despite my raging fears, as I started to talk to God, to actively participate in community life, and to make friends, I changed.

"We've Been Praying for You All Year"

After about ten months at Cenacolo, I began to experience an old emotion. It felt like jealousy. The parents of other young men were coming to see their sons, but no one was coming to see me—my family didn't even know where I was. I hadn't had any contact with them in all those wasted years. During the first few months I spent in the community, my mind cleared, and I realized that I loved them.

I felt so sorry for what I had done to my family that I wanted to get in touch with them—especially my father—and ask for forgiveness; but I simply did not know the way to go about it. Writing a letter wouldn't work, because I had written many letters from prison, always promising big things. I had deceived them thousands of times.

I eventually confessed my desire to my older friends in the community, and one of them told me, "Listen, friend. If you truly want it, if you really have this big wish to make up with your family, get up at two o'clock in the morning, go into the chapel, and kneel before Christ in the tabernacle. Pray and believe."

I asked him if I could go and pray during the day instead. "Why the heck would I get up at two in the morning?"

He laughed. "Hey friend, you've got to understand that you have to make some sacrifices to bear fruit."

I couldn't understand that, but day by day, my wish grew stronger and stronger. I started getting up at two to pray for my intention, but I didn't believe anything would happen. I thought I would die before my father would ever make peace with me.

Not long after my night prayers began, I was sitting in a workshop, learning from a community member how to draw icons, when another man in the room said, "Cuke, some pilgrims from Split are here, so please go and give them a tour of our community. Explain to them our program—how we live, how we work, and how we rebuild ourselves." I agreed and walked toward the refectory, opened the door, and looked around. The first head I saw among the visitors seated around the room was . . . my father's.

That was the hardest moment of my life. My father turned his head and saw me. He had learned where I was. I had no courage to look him in the eye—I couldn't even move from the door. I stared at the floor, with a rush of painful thoughts firing through my mind. I felt so embarrassed and ashamed. I wanted to run, but I knew there would be no more running. All my life, I had run from myself; this time, I had to stay. I had waited and longed for this moment, but now that it was here, I felt tormented.

My father saw the state I was in. He got up from his chair, walked over to me, and extended his hand. He started to cry. I reached out a trembling hand and started to cry, too. And then we hugged and kissed each other. We spent the next few hours walking around the grounds together, crying, unable to say a word.

At the end of our visit, I told him, "Dad, you are not to hope for anything. I am here, and I will work hard to stay here. I will work hard to become normal, to become a member of the family again. But you know how many times I have deceived you. I could go back into the streets and start taking drugs again. So don't hope. But I'm going to try. I'm going to try to take all the bad I did and pay it back three times over in goodness. Please pray for me, and I'll pray for you."

My father, who I thought never prayed, said, "We've been praying for you all year." And he embraced me tightly.

As difficult as the encounter was, the hope I saw in my father's eyes gave me the strength and renewed motivation to continue my way in the community. And every six months, my father and stepmother came to visit, bringing with them my brother's greetings.

After living in the Cenacolo community for about two and a half years, I began to entertain thoughts of leaving. I allowed myself to be encouraged to stay another eight months, and then at age thirty-three, I left. But after thirteen years away from Split, I didn't want to return home, so I asked the Franciscan priests in Medjugorje if they would find me work.

I Wanted to Get Married and Have a Family

The first job the priests landed for me was in the public bathrooms next to St. James Church in Medjugorje. If someone had told me while I was a drug addict that I would take a job in a public bathroom, I would have killed that person. But now, when they offered me that job, I felt so happy. I grabbed it with both hands. In addition to saving my life, the Cenacolo community had helped me to understand that no honest job is shameful, and every job should be handled responsibly and with good intentions.

After a couple of months, a desire grew within me to meet a girl. I wanted to get married and fulfill a lifelong dream of having a family—having others to sacrifice for and to love. However, wishes were one thing and reality quite another. I knew I was marked as a drug addict. Bosnia and Herzegovina, being very conservative in a godly way, would want its daughters united with the best husbands and sons-in-law possible. I was older, tattooed and scarred with a bullet in my head, no teeth, and no hair—and I worked scrubbing toilets. It wasn't going to be easy.

Yet I grew to have many friends, male and female, and all went well, except that women were letting me know they wanted nothing more than friendship. I was persistent, however. I prayed for my wish, and one day, as I was working in the public bathroom, I noticed a woman passing by.

To me, she was an icon of perfection. Her name was Katarina, and she was fourteen years younger than me. Somehow I got to know her. I learned that she wasn't from Medjugorje but had come from the Czech Republic to go on a pilgrimage for a month praying to God. That was the kind of wife I wished to have. But it was only a wish.

Katarina decided to stay in Medjugorje a while longer to discern whether or not she was called to be a Carmelite nun. For about eight months, I was like a puppy at her heels. She told me several times, in several ways, to leave her alone: "Maybe we can get together for coffee once in a while, but don't suffocate me" . . . "I'll never have you for my husband or my boyfriend" . . . "Look at yourself. You're covered with scars from knife wounds and tattoos, you're too old, and you have a dent in your head."

Undaunted, I persisted. "I'm looking for a woman," I told her.

"I will pray for you," she replied, while saying to God in the same breath, "Please, Lord, let it not be me."

"This Person Is You"

During this time, I received a promotion and began to do more difficult physical work, first sweeping and cleaning around the church, then sanding down and varnishing the hundreds of wooden benches inside and outside of St. James Church. I was having problems from back surgery that I'd had while in the community, and I ended up in the hospital again. I hadn't wanted to tell the Franciscan priests about the trouble with my spine, afraid they wouldn't let me stay in the work force. Considering my health and my past, employment was out of the question without their help. The Franciscans, upset with me for not telling them about my back pain, decided to give me another promotion. They took me into the parish office and asked me to handle the money that came in from the church collections.

Their trust in me did more than almost anything else to fully heal me. When someone asked them if I was trustworthy, Father Slavko, a beloved priest of Medjugorje, now deceased, whom I loved and admired greatly, answered, "I would trust this man with all of Mostar" [a nearby city].

All the while, I fought for Katarina with flowers and compliments, wanting to get closer to her and get her to like me, while she reminded me I was a habit that bored her. She later confessed that she actually liked the attention, because it felt very strange to her if I didn't come around during the week. At the time, however, she couldn't admit to herself that she missed me.

After eight months of pursuing Katarina, I traveled to Germany for a christening of a friend's baby and met a woman there. I had no thought of hooking up with her, but before I left, she let me know that if I pursued her, we could be together.

So I returned to Medjugorje with two women on my mind.

One day, I went to visit Katarina in the house where she was living. As she stood in front of the sink, doing dishes, I gave her a few compliments, but she still acted very cold. Then I said to her, "I've lost a lot of time with you, and I see that I am still getting nowhere. In Germany, I met a girl who is interested in me. Perhaps marriage is in her plans, so I will most likely go to Germany. I'll give my employer notice, and I'll probably be leaving soon."

When Katarina heard this, her face turned red. She threw down the plate in her hand and ran into the bedroom. "Aha!" I thought.

Shortly before I had stopped by that day, she had decided to pursue becoming a nun at a convent in Medjugorje and was planning to go there in a week to explore life as a sister. Realizing that I might leave for Germany at any time, she knew she needed to search God for what she should do. So she climbed to the top of Mount Krizevac, a sacred mountain in Medjugorje with a cross at its summit, where many miracles have occurred.

When Katarina arrived at the cross, God showed her her life, like a film before her eyes. She saw how short, angry, and rejecting she had been toward me. Then she thought of all the nice things I had done for her. She recalled how she had seen me treat others, especially orphaned children and the elderly. And she realized that in her head, she had rejected my exterior, but in her heart, she loved my interior.

Katarina then said to the Mother of God, "If Cuke approaches me and asks, 'Do you have something to tell me?'—I will tell him how I feel in my heart and what happened to me here on Mount Krizevac."

The next day, I asked Katarina to go out with me and some friends, and when we were in a café, I placed my hand on her knee, looked at her, and knowing nothing of her promise to Mary, I asked, "Do you want to tell me something?"

She whispered to me that she would like to talk, but later, not immediately. I responded, "Not later. Now." So we left the café and sat in my car.

Speaking in the third person, Katarina said that there was a man whom a certain young woman really didn't like, but didn't hate either. He was boring, not her type, and she never thought she could have a boyfriend or a husband like him. Then Katarina explained what had happened to this woman when she was praying on the mountaintop. Katarina paused, taking a deep breath. Then she continued: "I realized then that this person . . . I loved him in my heart . . . And this person is you. Now I am sorry for all the times I was saying 'no' while my heart was saying something else."

"Listen," I said to her, "that thing that happened in Germany wasn't really serious. So, why don't the two of us try going together?" She agreed and entered into the relationship, at first hesitantly but later with greater resolve and comfort.

After about a year, Katarina went to stay in the Cenacolo community in Italy for two months, simply to get closer to me, to understand my struggles, and to see the kind of place where I had spent my time and come to know God.

When she returned, we married in Medjugorje. My father sold a small apartment he owned and shared the money with my brother and me. This gift allowed me to build a home of my own on the outskirts of Medjugorje.

I worked hard directing a small community for rehabilitating drug addicts, and then I helped manage a store in Medjugorje. Recently, I decided to trust God with a talent he has given me for painting icons—a skill I learned from the community —and I began to sell them.

Katarina and I make a meager but happy living. Finances are a worry, and sometimes, with three kids, there isn't enough to eat. But that is when God sends somebody to help us, and for another day, we manage.

Now that most everyone in Medjugorje knows me, people consistently ask me to help them or their loved ones with their drug problems. And I offer the best advice I can, referring them to Cenacolo or other rehabilitation communities— whatever program will suit them best.

God Has Blessed Me

Just recently, I joined a free program that offered injections of interferon to support liver regeneration in people who have hepatitis C—a condition for which there is treatment but no known cure. Preliminary tests were required to check the condition of my liver, and when I returned to get my results, the doctor extended his hand to me. Taken aback, I was afraid to shake it. But he smiled at me and said, "We don't detect any hepatitis in you at all." God had granted me a miracle.

Not so long ago psychiatrists diagnosed me with paranoid schizophrenia and severe depression. At my worst, I was a hateful, aggressive, and dangerous man. I threatened people's lives and took from them whatever I could. I was a madman who existed in a sleepless nightmare—a wandering, decaying skeleton, wracked with hepatitis and severe malnutrition. Yet God always loved me. Just one hellish night on the floor of a derelict building, when I admitted my guilt with true sorrow and called out to the Mother of God, allowed the doors of grace to open.

My tattoos are no longer a mystery to me: the cross on top of a mountain and the hands in prayer holding the rosary over my heart. By the cross I have been saved, and, as if that weren't enough, God has blessed me with good health, sanity, a wife, and a family.

When I cried out to Mary, she listened to me—to every word of my prayer: "Mother of God, please take me up to yourself. Do something to change this poor life of mine. Extend your arms, I beg you." And she did. She truly did.

> Dear children, I am your mother and I warn you this time is a time of temptation. Satan is trying to find emptiness in you, so he can enter and destroy you. Do not surrender! I will pray with you. Do not pray just with your lips, but pray with the heart. In this way prayer will obtain victory!
>
> —Mary's message of July 4, 1988, from *Medjugorje Day by Day*

FOR PRAYERFUL REFLECTION

In Goran's life, we see an echo of a demoniac who lived in Jesus' time, a man so crazed and tortured that he cried out day and night and bruised himself with stones. Living but not alive, he walked among the tombs in the land of the Gerasenes.

> They came to the other side of the sea, to the territory of the Gerasenes. When [Jesus] got out of the boat, at once a man from the tombs who had an unclean spirit met him. The man had been dwelling among the tombs, and no one could restrain

him any longer, even with a chain. In fact, he had
frequently been bound with shackles and chains,
but the chains had been pulled apart by him and
the shackles smashed, and no one was strong
enough to subdue him. Night and day among the
tombs and on the hillsides he was always crying out and bruising himself with stones. Catching sight of Jesus from a distance, he ran up and
prostrated himself before him, crying out in a loud
voice, "What have you to do with me, Jesus, Son of
the Most High God? I adjure you by God, do not
torment me!" (He had been saying to him, "Unclean spirit, come out of the man!") He asked him,
"What is your name?" He replied, "Legion is my
name. There are many of us." And he pleaded ear-
nestly with him not to drive them away from that
territory.

Now a large herd of swine was feeding there
on the hillside. And they pleaded with him, "Send
us into the swine. Let us enter them." And he let
them, and the unclean spirits came out and entered
the swine. The herd of about two thousand rushed
down a steep bank into the sea, where they were
drowned. The swineherds ran away and reported
the incident in the town and throughout the coun-
tryside. And people came out to see what had happened. As they approached Jesus, they caught sight
of the man who had been possessed by Legion, sitting there clothed and in his right mind.

—Mark 5:1–15

1. What about Goran's story most moved you? Why?

2. Like the Gerasene demoniac, Goran was written off by humanity. Is
   there a person, a place, a group of people, or a race or nationality
   that you have written off as hopeless, irredeemable, or too
   dangerous? Have you chosen not to pray for certain people because you've thought to yourself, "Why bother?"

3. Goran turned to drugs and the streets for comfort. When you feel emptiness inside of you, what do you turn to for comfort? What works? What doesn't?

4. Goran's father and stepmother prayed for him. The young man in jail and his mother rescued him from the streets. The couple in Medjugorje made sure he got a ride to the Cenacolo community, where the people and program guided his soul. The Franciscan priests in Medjugorje encouraged and employed him. Even the axe murderer in the asylum spared Goran's life and helped him to survive, acting as an agent of God's will. Above all, his mother Mary in heaven interceded on his behalf before the throne of God, especially when he called out to her in true repentance. Who are the people, likely or unlikely, in heaven or on earth, whom God has used to help you on your journey toward him? How did they influence you or assist you?

5. Lying on the floor of the derelict building, having lost everything, Goran finally saw the truth of his past. Has a humbling moment ever clarified your sinfulness before God? If so, how did it feel? How did God respond? Did it change you?

6. What does Goran's story say about the kind of love and mercy that is Jesus and that lives in the heart of Mary? Do you believe that this love and mercy is there for you? Why or why not?

FAITH EXERCISE

Enter into prayer, and ask God to reveal to you one area in your life or heart about which you feel deep regret or shame—perhaps a memory, thought, habit, or sin that has distanced you from God.

Then close your eyes and lift up into the arms of Mary what has been revealed to you, asking for her touch of mercy and love upon you. Notice what she does. Notice your response.

Remain with Mary in prayer until you sense it is time to open your eyes.

TWO

JOHN

Driven by a need to be liked, a sad and lonely
young man is embraced by Mary
and discovers how deeply he is loved.

Growing up, I felt neglected. My mom and dad were good
people, but they didn't show much affection and were rarely
home. I was lonely and thought my parents didn't care if I existed or not. I'd often hide in the closet for hours and listen
to hear if anyone missed me, but no one ever noticed I was
gone.

From kindergarten through second grade, I lived with a
fear that when I arrived home after school, everyone—my
parents, sister, and two brothers—would be gone. My parents
were good people, so I figured they would leave me plenty of
food, but would just leave one day and forget to take me with
them.

These feelings of abandonment created a hunger and thirst
in me to be seen and loved and held. At Saint Philip's Church,
near where I grew up in Southern California, I would look up
and stare at the sanctuary wall, which was covered with a beautiful painting of God the Father in the clouds: a white-bearded

old man who looked like Santa Claus. Up until about second grade, whenever I was alone outside, I looked up at the sky and talked to God, who I figured must be in the clouds. At those times, I felt his presence and loving encouragement. I was very shy and lonely, so God became my friend.

God, for me, was a lot like my dad. He took us to church; all my friends loved him; and he seemed to have everything I wanted. He had a reputation for doing good works in the community, such as helping the poor, the elderly, and juvenile delinquents.

When I was five years old, my parents divorced, and my mom remarried. After the divorce, I didn't talk to God anymore. I felt disconnected, with no control and no rudder, like a leaf floating down a river. To cope with life, I watched about five or six hours of TV a day for the next twenty years. I also became intent on stacking up achievements and popularity in order to be like my dad and get some kind of attention; but what I truly wanted was to be loved.

I Learned to Hide My Weakness

I took on the example of my dad as a working model of faith, and God disappeared. I thought that what faith really boiled down to was being popular and good. But being both was too difficult, so I chose popular.

By the time I entered middle school, I didn't care about other people and openly made fun of anyone socially awkward. I was cool. I knew God wasn't too happy with my behavior, though, so I hid from him by not paying attention during Catechism classes and by daydreaming and joking around at Mass.

I was very well liked. In middle school, I was good in sports and in school, and I had lots of friends. I figured that by the time I approached my dad's age, I would be satiated with popularity, and everything would be in place.

Then I went from a small middle school to a big high school, the same high school my dad had attended, where everyone told me I was just like him. What I found out, though, was that I was not like my dad.

High school academics were hard for me; I could barely manage. I could have played sports, but at that point I felt that unless I was going to be the best, I shouldn't even try. If I shared my gifts and didn't prove to be good enough, then my weaknesses would be exposed, and I would know for sure that I was, in truth, useless.

I didn't have a single friend throughout high school. Not doing sports, I didn't have any sports friends. Wanting to be good, I didn't hang out with the troublemakers and the kids taking drugs. There was no way I was going to hang out with the nerds. I existed in a horribly lonely space. During recess, I walked around as though I had a destination; but, in reality, I had nowhere to go and no one to be with.

Compounding the loneliness was my fear and embarrassment over ever admitting my failures to God or to my family, especially my dad. What if they thought I was a dork and didn't like me? I learned to hide my weaknesses from others and from myself. Foolishly, I hoped that God would overlook me, too, while at the same time I worried he would do just that. On top of it all, I felt a sense of hopelessness and despair. My dream was not going to happen. Many times, I wished I were dead. I felt as though I was drifting away, and one day I would be gone.

That was my state of mind when, around my sophomore year at age sixteen, I went to Mass with my siblings and my dad. While they sat clustered in the middle of a pew, I sat at its end, physically and emotionally detached, in utter despair, almost to the point of wondering, "Why live?" Just before the "kiss of peace," when people shake hands and say to one another, "Peace be with you," I yelled to God internally with all my heart, "Give me peace!" In the next moment, I saw a homeless man in the corner of my eye, standing in a pew behind me. The church was full, but no one had wanted to sit next to him. I had never seen a homeless person before, but I knew his state by the way he looked and smelled. His face was red and unshaven, his hands big and rough, and his clothes dirty and brown.

I immediately felt drawn to this man. I walked over to him, held out my hand, and simply offered him peace. An incredible wave of serenity passed through me. As we shook hands, I felt God hugging me and the homeless man together. I sensed God revealing to me that this man was my brother, that we shared a kinship in being broken and outcasts; and I realized that God really loved him—and loved me. Through this homeless man, God was giving me special attention, that full attention I craved. With God's love and physical presence rushing through me, I felt like I had come home from a very long and tiring trip, and my parents were there to give me a big hug and to let me know I was safe. Our hands parted, and the homeless man looked into my eyes and said, "There are a lot of good people here, but you're the only one who understands the message of the Gospel today."

God Was Calling Me

After the encounter with the homeless man, I began to pray again. My high school teacher, Father DeLancey, told our class, "You just need to talk to God. Say 'hello,' and wait for him to respond." So I followed his advice. I fully expected I would hear God, and I did, in subtle words and impressions in my heart. He spoke to me, telling me he loved me in many different ways, and I thought of this as completely normal at the time.

A year later, when I was seventeen, this time of grace ended. One day, as I lay on my bed at home, chatting with God nonchalantly, I asked him, "So God, what should I do? Should I be a fireman? A fighter pilot? Should I be a businessman, like my dad?" I rattled off many different professions, and then I stopped and said, "Well, God, what do you want me to do?"

And that was when God shocked me with a clear and challenging internal voice. He called me by name and said, "Johnny, I want you to forget about all these things. I want you to forget about what your parents want you to do, and follow me." Up until then, our dialogues were more casual, more encouraging, but in this one he confronted me. God was calling me to do something, and I was terrified.

I was afraid that he was calling me to leave my parents' house, to enter the priesthood; to be persecuted; to die; or, even worse in my opinion, to speak in front of people. Following God felt like an out-of-control choice, but I didn't dare say no. If I said anything negative to God, I figured he wouldn't like me anymore, so I stopped talking to him. I pretended that he hadn't said anything and I hadn't heard anything.

I stopped praying for ten years. I thought God was mad at me, and I refused to chat with him alone because then he might start talking to me again in a louder voice. I went to church only because I felt safe from him there.

I Walked a Fine Line

In college, I regained a sense of popularity, and again, I set off on a path of hope that I could become likeable. Those were exciting times, with lots of friends and laughter, but I also made a lot of mistakes. I lost my sensitivity toward others, toward the poor, the outcast. Wanting to be part of the gang, I walked a fine line between being good and being cool. I also started drinking too much and got involved in premarital sex, which ultimately led to disastrous consequences and served to add more pain to my wounds.

When I was twenty-one and in college, I started dating my first long-term girlfriend. She was the first person with whom I had intercourse. One night, near the end of our relationship, we were both overtaken by lust and had sex.

I went home and had a dream that night—a very clear vision of conception. It looked like a scene from a Nova television program. I saw a light, followed by a sperm connecting with an egg, which then exploded into life—with cells breaking up and multiplying everywhere. I sensed that the person created at that moment was a boy. I woke up and shared the dream with a friend who said, "Whoa, man. Be careful not to get her pregnant."

A few weeks later, my girlfriend called me up. All she said was, "I need to talk to you," but in my heart I knew she was pregnant. She came over, told me of the pregnancy, and said she was going to have an abortion. "I know what your opinion is," she added, "and I don't want to hear it." I felt numb and powerless.

She went and had the abortion. The experience passed like a bad dream we never spoke of. Then I blocked it out.

After the abortion and the end of that relationship, my heart hardened. I had many friends, but never close ones, and I entered into other sexual relationships, but didn't care about them much.

I Didn't Grow More Loving, and I Don't Know If I Really Helped Anybody

As the years passed, I grew nearer to following in my dad's footsteps—making my way in the world of sales, getting involved in different community volunteer activities—and becoming more and more miserable. I moved to San Francisco with a new job, selling phone systems. But I worked from my home in solitude, without friends again, in that same old place of loneliness.

Seeking comfort, I decided to become more active in my church, and as I did, the memory of God calling me to follow him began to gnaw at me. I still felt too afraid to sit down and truly listen to him, so to appease God, I got very involved in the church by volunteering, giving talks, and helping the poor.

But I was still trying to do things my way—still trying to stay in control of my life. It didn't work. I grew anxious and depressed and started to have panic attacks. In desperation, I began to pray again.

After working up the courage, I braced myself. I was going to talk to God directly. With a trembling heart, I asked him, "Hi . . . so . . . what did you mean when you said, 'Follow me'?" I almost winced because I thought he would respond right away and perhaps be angry. But I didn't hear anything back. After weeks of asking him and hearing nothing, I began to despair. Maybe God had given me a one-shot deal and had forgotten about me.

I soon realized that no matter what I did, if I didn't ultimately do what God had asked of me, my life was going to be fruitless. Thinking perhaps he was calling me to become a priest, I decided—with the help and encouragement of an acquaintance—to go to spiritual direction. I needed to discern God's calling.

In one of my sessions with my spiritual director, she had me imagine myself as a priest and asked me what it felt like. I saw myself surrounded by children, working with the poor, being a voice for them, serving them, and being in community with them; but I didn't see myself administering the Sacraments as a priest. In an effort to please God and be "good" at serving the poor, I decided to cover all my bases and volunteered for almost every ministry at my church, as well as at a homeless shelter for families where I began working with children.

At age twenty-eight, I reached a point of extreme frustration. As I became more involved in church and volunteer work, I felt less peaceful. I didn't grow more loving, and I don't know if I really helped anybody. From my dad's example, I had learned that if you did a lot of things well, you would be rewarded. But I was a drone, reaping misery. To be successful at sales, I had to be pushy and lie, and I could be mean. Even my good works enslaved me and did nothing to pull me out of my predicament.

I was becoming physically tired, with depression and anxiety. When my anxiety became unmanageable, I started taking Paxil, an antidepressant, and seeing a Christian therapist. I had reached my limits. I couldn't do any more than I was doing, and what I was doing wasn't enough to quench the least bit of my thirst to be loved.

One day, while I was praying in a fetal position on my bed, I finally flung up my hands to God in desperation and said, "God, everything that I've done has turned into shit. I can't do anything on my own. It all turns bad. Whatever you want me to do, I'll do. If you want me to be a homeless person, a priest, or a persecuted prophet, I'll be that—anything. Whatever you want me to be is infinitely better than the emptiness I feel now. And, God, whatever you want me to be or do, you will have to make it happen because everything that I do turns to crap."

Within two weeks, I quit my job and got a new position, at a 75 percent pay cut, working with homeless families and children at the homeless shelter where I volunteered. Finally, I had found a place where I felt at home—with the outcasts.

Jesus, This Is Who I Am

With the help of spiritual direction, I continued to reflect on the moment when I was seventeen and God called me to follow him. It scared me to think that out of billions of people on this earth, he had called me by name. But this being so, I knew he must care about me, even though I had let him down multiple times. God reinforced this when I put into practice something Saint Paul said in his letter to the Ephesians: ". . . everything exposed by the light becomes visible, for everything that becomes visible is light" (5:11b-14a). I decided to expose my sins to Jesus. When thoughts or feelings of road rage, lust, or judgment came over me, I said, "Jesus, I want you to know this about me. This is who I am." I fully expected him to come to me with the merciless judgment and shame I normally gave myself, but instead, he gave me a healing wave of peace— every time.

I began to trust God again. Slowly, I went from a faith of doing to a faith of relationship. Most people who knew me thought, "Nice kid, nice boy," while my rage, bitterness, judgment, and other sins ate at me inside. Only Jesus knew who I really was. He became my only authentic friend.

Until then, I did not have much of a relationship with anyone. I was playing the roles of good son, good church person, and good social worker, so I didn't know who I was—my different personas limited my capacity to know myself, and I wasn't very interested in knowing other people, only in making sure they saw my persona as likeable. My heart was disconnected, but when I stopped hiding from Jesus and lifted up to him the dark sides of my life, the moment they happened, his mercy changed me.

A couple years into that process, I had a dream that pointed to this conversion. In the dream I met a prophet, an old man standing on a platform preaching about Jesus, saying that the devil was real and that he was trying to destroy us. I joined the small crowd of people standing around him, and as I listened, I believed him and became his disciple. Then he said, "If you believe this message, then you need to start preaching it," so in the dream, I started preaching to non-Christian friends in my life, which I never did, for fear of their reaction.

As I began to tell them and other small groups of people to repent because Satan was real, I realized that Satan was now aware of me. Before then, he paid me no notice, but now that I was speaking the truth, he wanted to destroy me. Suddenly everyone disappeared, and I was left standing face-to-face with Satan. He looked like an ordinary man with curly black hair—no pitchforks, horns, or red tail. There was nothing distinguishing about him except for his qualities of evil and power. With a smug and disdainful look on his face he said to me, "God is not going to save you. Even if God cared about you, which he doesn't, because you're just one person among billions, he could not overpower me. I'm just as strong as he is."

I felt an urge inside of me to respond as I normally did in dreams, to posture, to pretend I possessed special powers, to rail at him like a loud prophet—in order to appear capable and wonderful—a set-up that suited him perfectly, because I just went nowhere. But instinctively, as I stood before him, I knew he could destroy me. Shaken, I thought, "Out of billions of people, is God really aware of me?" Then, in that moment, I remembered that Jesus had never left me. I knew he would protect me. I didn't know how powerful Satan was, but I knew that Jesus defeated Satan because of the Resurrection and because of my experiences of his healing mercy. My only thought of hope was the Lord, so I fell down on my knees, and in a deep, guttural prayer, said, "Jesus, save me!" Then I collapsed forward into a fetal position, and with my whole body and my whole will, I held on to his legs in faith. "I'm going to stay here and hold on to you Jesus," I said, "even if Satan kills me. I'm going to hold on to you until I get to heaven."

Satan stood still in front of me. I knew he could kill me, but I also knew that because I was clinging to Jesus, I was not going to hell if he did. Then a beautiful feeling of peace overtook me. Jesus had responded to my cry and saved me. I looked up and saw Satan. He smiled, shook his head, and walked away, but in his look I saw him say, "You're mine. I'll get you later." Then I woke up. I was sitting on the couch with a pillow clenched in my arms and tears in my eyes.

With that dream, my persona broke. I came to find the peace of Christ in my utter defeat—a victory far beyond what I could ever have achieved or imagined. I didn't have to put up a powerful façade because the façade was not going to save me. Jesus was.

"Be Subordinate to One Another in Reverence to Christ"

My relationship with God was deepening, but I still struggled through my relationships with people. I dated a gal for a couple years, and although I tried to make the relationship work, I didn't emotionally invest in it at all. Shortly before we parted ways, she gave me a tape of a Protestant preacher, who explained the beauty of the sacrament of marriage, using Paul's letter to the Ephesians, chapter 5. Before that, I didn't think I would ever show interest in marriage, but the tape explained the sacred nature of the sacrament by using Saint Paul's words in an appealing, nonsexist way. Focusing on the line, "Be subordinate to one another in reverence to Christ," the preacher explained that marriage could be a journey toward Christ, and I saw, for the first time, that God was calling me to marriage as a vocation—but not with this young woman. The tape gave me clarity to end that relationship, and my next girlfriend, Christine, became my wife.

A month into dating her, I had a dream in which I saw a bride and groom at a wedding Mass. A viciously demonic alligator, intent on bloody revenge, planned to tear them apart with his jaws, but I knew the woman was going to destroy it, and this gave me a sense of peace. The alligator, fuming with rage, began to charge at her and her husband-to-be. She stepped forward with a cup of Christ's blood that she had in her hand, threw the consecrated wine over the alligator, and it disappeared.

I knew that my bride would be instrumental in healing me and bringing me closer to God, but I had no idea how.

Medjugorje Was Both Difficult and Transformative

Just after our wedding, my wife sensed we were called to go on a pilgrimage to Medjugorje, where the Virgin Mary is appearing. I struggled quite a bit with the idea of going, because I hadn't grown up with any kind of Marian influence, didn't pray the rosary, and my entire faith life had centered around Jesus. I felt very fearful of having anyone, even Mary, stand between us.

Saint Paul's line from Ephesians 5 helped me to begrudgingly submit to the pilgrimage: "Be subordinate to one another in reverence to Christ."

On Christmas Day, at midnight, we were off. On the plane ride to Medjugorje, I wrote in my journal to Mary—the first time I had ever addressed her. Although I didn't think it was very fair of me, since I hadn't thought much about the Mother of God, I asked her for a miracle. I wanted a sign that she was there, that Medjugorje was real.

Medjugorje was both difficult and transformative for me. My first challenge came suddenly. Our pilgrimage leader told the group on our second day of the trip that she had a surprise in store for us. That evening she walked us over to the visionary Marija's house and said we were going to be present for a small, private apparition in a tiny chapel attached to Marija's home. I became quiet and terrified.

I wanted to believe the visionaries. But I was afraid that any relationship I might develop with Mary could rock my faith and my relationship with Jesus. The risk was too great. Furthermore, what if nothing happened? Suddenly, I realized that I was afraid of this as well. What if I were praying only a few feet from the Virgin Mary, the Queen of Peace, and I felt nothing? What would that say about my faith? What should I do? As I sat and prayed in the chapel, my anxieties and fears slowly began to build and build. Just moments before the apparition, I panicked and thought, "Run! Get out of here!" Then a soft voice inside me said, "Go to Jesus." Of course! I had always been able to go to Jesus. He was my rock, my salvation. I could always trust in him. So I got down on my knees and prayed to him. At 5:40 p.m., in the middle of a communal rosary, all grew quiet, and Marija had her apparition. I felt safe. Staying close to him, I knew that nothing could harm me.

Later, I reflected on the experience. "Where did that voice come from?" Perhaps it was Mary. After all, those who prayed to Mary said that she always leads one to Jesus. Still troubled, I held onto that thought.

This Is How You Hold My Son

By the third day of the pilgrimage, I began to wonder why I was there at all. I felt like an outsider among a group of devout, wonderful, faith-filled people. They had accepted Mary's gift of motherhood, but for some reason, I couldn't shake my feelings of distrust in her. Humbled, I realized perhaps my faith was not so strong. I told Christine that perhaps the rosary just wasn't for me. Still, as my wife pointed out, maybe praying the rosary was not simply about feeling but about obedience. If I believed what the visionaries were saying, which I did, then I was called to pray the rosary. I decided to ask Jesus to help me to get to know his mother Mary, and to help me to understand her whole purpose.

That night, two women in our group, Natalie and Alicia, invited Christine and me to hike up Cross Mountain early the next day. Apparently, Mary prays to Jesus at the foot of a large cross on top of this mountain in Medjugorje at five each morning. Initially, I declined, but then I thought to myself, "I might not have a good relationship with Mary, but one thing I have in common with her is the desire to pray at the foot of the cross to her Son."

The hike itself was incredible. Christine, Natalie, Alicia, and I set out early in the dark morning, at about quarter to four. As we started the climb, my companions, as I expected, pulled out their rosary beads—"Hail Mary . . ." they chanted. I kept my hands defiantly in my pockets and began praying quietly to Jesus. Shortly after that, Christine began wheezing and couldn't continue praying out loud. On behalf of my wife, I picked up my rosary and decided to pray it—just this once.

For the first time, I felt engaged. The rosary had a purpose for me now. Since Christine had a relationship with Mary, I knew Mary would like me to pray it for her. With my love for Christine in my heart, I prayed each mystery of the rosary; and as the other two women became tired, I tried to pray the rosary even harder for them as well. At one point, I even began to lead the rosary.

An incredible energy surged through me as I bolted up the mountain. I felt amazed by Alicia and Natalie's faith and commitment.

Tired and out of breath, they continued up the mountainside, gasping out the prayers, intent on reaching the summit. As we neared the top, time was running out. We had to keep moving. Christine and I climbed past our fatigued companions. I felt inspired.

Reaching the cross at exactly five, I fell down at the foot of it, sensing Mary right next to me, and I prayed to Jesus. Christine stayed ten feet back. She was, I learned later, praying that Mary might intercede before God and show me a sign. Bent over on one knee, I felt quietly serene. Then I saw a sudden flash of light brighten the entire sky and illuminate the mountainside. It looked similar to a bolt of lightning, except that it was a straight, vertical line, amidst no clouds, no rain, and no thunder.

Christine opened her eyes just after it happened and asked me, "Did you just see something? Was there a flash of light?" I couldn't answer her because I was starting to cry. The miracle had taken my breath away, and I sensed Mary say to my heart, "I'm here with you, and I am inviting you into a relationship with me."

Natalie and Alicia arrived at the top of the mountain five minutes later. They hadn't seen the light illuminate the sky and cover the mountainside. Awestruck and humbled, I realized that perhaps the sign was meant just for me—that Mary, who knew my doubts, might be reaching out to me. Reflecting on my climb up the mountain, I also realized how Jesus had answered my prayers by giving me an insight into Mary's role. I understood that just as I prayed for my wife when she could not pray, Mary prays for us and with us when we get tired, distracted, or neglectful in prayer.

That night, in the freezing cold, Christine and I made another climb, this time up Apparition Hill where a sea of people, praying the rosary in different languages, waited for an apparition to the visionary Ivan. I started feeling angst once again, so I crouched down and clasped my hands together, clinging tightly to Jesus for a sense of peace. Growing more and more uncomfortable, I decided to place my hands down on the ground, and just as I did, the crowd hushed. The apparition began. And I heard an internal voice say, "Don't let go." Then, guided by a gentle force, I put my hands back together and noticed that I was no longer clinging to Jesus, but instead was poised, as though holding a baby in my arms, in a soft, gentle embrace. It was as if Mary were saying, "No, my dear one. You needn't be afraid. This is how you hold my Son."

The day before we were scheduled to leave, I smelled roses on the cross that I wore around my neck, and no rose perfume or roses were present. I had never smelled Mary's mystical scent of roses before, and I kept bringing my cross up to my nose to test whether I had imagined it.

I received so many graces in Medjugorje that Satan was going to make sure I didn't return with them. At the airport, I began to doubt everything—the scent of roses, Mary's messages to me, and the miracle at the cross. When I arrived home, I wasn't sure what I believed anymore. Christine wanted me to give a talk with her at our parish about our pilgrimage, but I wanted nothing to do with it. To numb myself, I sat on the couch drinking beer and watching television for three days.

I wanted to hide and deny my beliefs because Jesus and Mary were leading me to the cross, where I met up with my greatest fear—the fear of being disliked, rejected, and abandoned. They were asking me to reveal to the world who I really was, a Christian.

I Didn't Have to Hide Anymore

A couple weeks after coming back from Medjugorje, I braced myself for a trip to Aspen, Colorado, where I would visit some of my old college buddies. I counted on Mary's prayers to help me pick up the cross I didn't want to carry, while still keeping her at a safe distance, in case she might interfere with my relationship with her Son.

In Aspen, one of my friends, right at the start, said something condescending about my being Christian. "So I hear you've really gone off the deep end with this Christian stuff," he said. "It looks like you've gone kooky on us. I'm expecting a halo to float out of your head any moment now."

He became the antagonist of the four-day trip. At every opportunity, he verbally attacked me in front of others and made snide comments. And every single moment I had free—if I was walking to the car or to the bathroom—I said the rosary. To my amazement, I didn't feel afraid. I responded sincerely and thoughtfully to his insults, without getting defensive or downplaying my faith and my involvement in the Church, as I normally did. At one point, he sat down across from me and became very aggressive, asking me one question after another, trying to put holes in my faith; but I felt filled with the Holy Spirit. Gradually, one, two, then three people sat around our table. Then finally, the whole group sat down and listened as I preached the Word, challenging this or that person gently, and talking about my own experiences of faith. "That might have been you," he said, "but stuff like that wouldn't happen to me."

"If you want these experiences," I told him, "you're not going to get them by talking to me about it. If you want a relationship with God, with Jesus, you'll have to ask him to be in your life, and then you'll find him there. In fact, he's already there."

Then he backed down and said, "You know what? I'm afraid. I don't want to change my life."

I had feared that by sharing my faith, I would find myself alone with no one to understand me. But I found that by being true and bringing out the light, I had split the room. I could see very clearly that half the people there were already searching for God, and half were trying to avoid God, but God was working with all of them. While in one respect stating who I was in my faith did cut me off from some, in another, I started to have a more authentic relationship with every person in that room. I didn't have to hide anymore. Some of them were even amazingly thankful. At the end of the trip, the host, who was not a Christian, said, "In the many years we've been doing this, we've never had this type of spirit in the group. This was the first real conversation we've had that cut through our surface level talk. And that's thanks to you."

God continued calling me to be authentic. I took that into my family, and I took that into my workplace. I gave a parish talk with Christine on Medjugorje, and it went well. I became more fearless in my faith. This can be credited to two things: my trust in Jesus and my extra assurance that Mary would always be present for me, even if I didn't fully trust her. My primary drive to be liked had kept me in a prison. Without the love of Jesus and support of Mary, I wouldn't have had the confidence to risk being unloved, to risk being free.

My Son Would Be Fifteen Now

After a year of marriage, my wife, in her prayers, sensed that Mary was calling me to a Rachel's Vineyard Retreat for further healing around my college girlfriend's abortion. I wanted to believe it was resolved because I had gone to confession. "Why should I dig up the past and create a situation to make myself feel bad," I wondered, "when I've put away the abortion and don't have to deal with it anymore?" I also feared I would feel very out of place in a room with a bunch of weeping women. I dragged my feet and didn't want to go. Once again, Saint Paul's line, "Be subordinate to one another in reverence to Christ," helped me submit to my wife. Perhaps God was using her for his purposes.

The first day of the weekend retreat I felt awkward, even though I was not the only man there. But my uneasiness turned into grace. Shocked to discover I had any emotion at all around the abortion, I found that a great sadness was present inside of me, and I turned out to be the one crying more than most of the women. Asking for forgiveness and asking the child to be in my life again greatly healed me. I discovered I could relate to him, even ask him to pray for me. My son would be fifteen now. I named him Joshua.

I went from the denial of my own parenthood to the recognition of who and what I am, not only as Christine's husband but also as Joshua's father. I was allowed the opportunity to begin grieving the loss of my child. Healing from the abortion, I learned, was going to take more than just the confession of a sin. A precious life that was a gift to me, that I was a steward for, was never allowed to live.

By denying the child's life, my part in creating it and taking it, and by simply talking about the abortion as a sin, I had been disconnecting from my true identity. This is something I see with other men. Women sometimes grieve abortion more because the act is part of their body. For men, it is easier to deny the act and any responsibility for it. And when we men do that, we suffer without even knowing why we are in pain. Problems like my anxiety disorder, my outbursts of anger, and my having to take Paxil came after the abortion and were tied to it. We cannot disconnect from our feelings of loss and feelings about others without disconnecting from who we are as human beings. That is the price we pay. My child is part of who I am.

During the retreat, I reconnected with Joshua. By being able to grieve in this way, I was able to retrieve a part of my humanity that was tied to this child. It was a mistake to kill my child.

I wrote a letter to him to apologize:

> My dear little Joshua,
> You are probably wondering where I've been, why I left you behind to die, and why I didn't even bother to think about you these many years. The answers to these questions do not come so easy. The truth is that I was a coward for not speaking up for you twelve years ago now, and I have continued to be a coward, running away from my sin. It gives me comfort to know that you might be with Jesus right now as I write this letter to you, but it saddens me to know that I will never see you in this lifetime. I know that you would have been a special boy, a beautiful gift from God. I'm sorry that I did not see that then. I was afraid, afraid of what people might think if they found out that your mom was pregnant, afraid of your mom's anger if I questioned her.

I put the guilt of our sin on her, and I was wrong for that. She was young and afraid like me. Like me, she didn't want to believe that she was killing her own son. We were both at fault. I'm sorry for my part, and I'm sorry for blaming your mom. I pray that she may also one day see you in heaven.

As for me, I humbly ask for your forgiveness. How could you forgive me? I would understand if you didn't. I hope it is not too late to turn things around for us. I have been a terrible father. How could I contemplate bringing more children into the world without first reconciling with my oldest son?

I don't know if there is any gift that I could share with you that could compare with the gift you have received in being with Jesus for all eternity, but I would like to reach out to you, to hug you as my son, to share my heart with you. I would like it if you could give me a second chance to be the father that I wasn't for so many years. I missed seeing you as a baby, seeing your first steps, comforting you in your fears, laughing with you, disciplining you, teaching you, loving you.

God willing, I would like to see you. Maybe God would grant me this request before I die. To be able to hold my oldest son in this lifetime would be a great gift. If you would like to see me, ask Jesus. I'm sure he will grant you this request. I know he loves you very much. Please ask him. It would mean a lot to me.

I promise I will continue to pray for your mom, and I hope that you will keep me and my wife in your prayers. I know I wouldn't have had the courage to try to contact you if it wasn't for her. She means the world to me. We are both hoping that we can have children one day, God willing. We would like you to be included in our family. Please think about it, and let us know.

Love always.
Your dad,
John

For the Very First Time, I Felt Connected to Mary

My last relationship that still needed repair was with Mary. Despite all of the help she had given me, I continued to fear that she would get in the way of my bond with Jesus. I was obeying all her messages from Medjugorje, and I still do, by praying the rosary every day, fasting on bread and water on Wednesdays and Fridays, reading the Bible, going to confession once a month, and receiving the eucharist—and all of this was helping me to grow and mature in my faith. But I did all these good deeds for her, like I had done good deeds for my mom, my dad, and God—without engaging in a real relationship.

When I went to see my new spiritual director, she said, "I think that Mary is now calling you into a deeper relationship." Her words didn't strike me as much as her awareness of Mary's presence as she said this. She even began to tear up. "Mary wants you to come to know her and her Son through the depths of your heart," she continued, "like the disciples in the Emmaus story came to know Jesus when they said to each other, 'Were not our hearts on fire while he spoke to us on the way . . . ?' [Luke 24:32]."

I decided to go on a silent weekend retreat, directed by a Jesuit priest, and dedicate it to Mary. Before my first spiritual direction session with the priest, before I told him anything about myself, he walked into the retreat center bookstore, and while showing me around, spontaneously bought me a book called *Hearts on Fire*. I opened the book, and the very first line was from the Emmaus story: "Were not our hearts on fire?"

On retreat, I intentionally remembered and showed Mary scenes from my life, in the hope of having a deeper relationship with her. I sat and listened to anything she might want to tell me, but heard only silence. The Jesuit priest helped me to see that part of the reason I couldn't connect with Mary was because my vision of her reflected how she is often depicted in art. I saw Jesus with the disciples and on the cross, acting real; but I saw Mary, standing upright, in a blue robe, in the clouds—a powerful, sometimes stern figure—acting surreal. I told the priest that my fears of her, by this point, had turned into nightmares. Soon after returning from Medjugorje, I'd woken up one night with a start, thinking I'd seen her at the foot of the bed. Too afraid to scream, I began thrashing around, kicking off the bed covers and cutting my hand on the alarm clock. In another nightmare, I'd dreamt that I'd woken up and looked into a mirror to see Mary standing right behind me. Frozen with fear, I couldn't speak, move, or breathe.

The priest recommended I meditate on a passage from the Bible that gave more of a human aspect to Mary. I chose the depiction of Mary in John 19, where Jesus gave her to the disciple, John, at the foot of the cross. My intent was to observe Mary in a very painful human experience of loss, not in any way in a position of power.

I went off to pray by myself. Closing my eyes, I entered into a meditation, placing myself at the foot of the cross with Mary, but this time I wasn't in Medjugorje. I was in Calvary. I looked beside me and saw Mary, hunched over, overwhelmed and crying. She was wearing black, with a shawl covering her head. I stood behind her, watching. I saw true human sadness in her huddled figure and felt a stirring in my heart, connecting mine to hers. I looked up at Jesus' eyes and face, and just as I did, he said to his mother, "Behold your son." Then he turned his head away from her to look right at me.

I broke down crying. I just felt loved. I hadn't anticipated that at all. I was simply there as a spectator. For the very first time, I felt connected to Mary, and I was able to suffer and to cry with her. I collapsed down by her side, put my arm around her, and we sobbed together.

When I look at Mary now, I begin to weep. I begin to have an emotional response. Before, I felt afraid of her; now I feel love for her, and I sense her love and support for me. Even though she had given me many experiences that could have led me to believe she was trustworthy, it wasn't until Jesus himself showed me that he was the one leading me to Mary that I trusted her.

Just last weekend, when I was sitting in a pew at church, terrified to get up and speak during a Mass on behalf of Catholic Charities, an overwhelming sense of peace descended upon me, and I looked up wondering where it came from. Everywhere around the church I started to see Mary. I looked up above me and saw her sculpted in the rafters, hunched over at the foot of the crucifixion. I looked to my left and saw her in agony, holding Jesus after he had been taken down from the cross. Then I looked up again and saw yet another image of her, extending her arms. I began to cry. I recognized that she was truly there, and that she would always be there for me, even after I die.

When I received the eucharist at that same Mass, I felt my heart burning with a sweet warmth inside my chest. This lasted for a while, giving me the most intense feeling of love in my heart I had ever experienced. The feeling even burned through my doubts that it was real.

Mary had led me to Jesus, and then, literally, my heart caught fire.

If you would abandon yourselves to me, you would not
even feel the passage from this life to the next. You would
begin to live the life of heaven on earth.

—Mary's message in 1986, from *Medjugorje Day by Day*

FOR PRAYERFUL REFLECTION

When John was a young boy, feeling alone and invisible, God
gave him friendship; when John was a teenager, pondering
his future, God gave him an answer: "Follow me"; when John
grew into adulthood, God gave him Mary, and challenged him
to unlock the riches of his heart, to share who he really was—to
go and make disciples.

> The eleven disciples went to Galilee, to the moun-
> tain to which Jesus had ordered them. When they
> saw him, they worshiped, but they doubted. Then
> Jesus approached and said to them, "All power
> in heaven and on earth has been given to me. Go,
> therefore, and make disciples of all nations, baptiz-
> ing them in the name of the Father, and of the Son,
> and of the holy Spirit, teaching them to observe all
> that I have commanded you. And behold, I am with
> you always, until the end of the age."
> —Matthew 28:16–20

1. When God asked John to follow him, John refused to pray for
    ten years and went to church only because he felt safe from God
    there. Has something God asked of you ever plunged you into par-
    alyzing fear? What was it? How did you avoid it or work through it?
    Was the fear lifted by the Lord's grace?

2. When John encountered the homeless man in church, a sweep-
    ing sense of God's presence came over them both. Have you ever

sensed the living God communicate to you through another person? Through the poor? Recollect what happened. How were you affected by this experience?

3. Actions that John most feared and resisted turned out to be his greatest triumphs, such as probing what God meant when he said, "Follow me," and traveling all the way to Medjugorje. These decisions demanded a leap of faith. Have you triumphed in taking a leap of faith in the past? Recall that experience, and notice what it evokes in you. What leap of faith is being asked of you now? How can past triumphs spur you toward what God may be asking of you?

4. Have you ever felt as though you just didn't and couldn't live up to God's standards? If so, how has this affected your thoughts and behaviors? How has God shown you his mercy on occasions when you felt more like an underperformer than a beloved, accepted child of God?

5. Could you relate to John's times of feeling lonely, forgotten, unwanted, and abandoned? If so, have you sensed God with you during those times?

6. Have fear or embarrassment ever kept you from sharing your Catholic faith? Can you name those fears? What might help you break through them?

FAITH EXERCISE

In his encyclical, *Redemptoris Missio* ("The Mission of Christ the Redeemer"), Pope John Paul II wrote: "It is the Spirit who impels us to proclaim the great works of God: 'For if I preach the Gospel, that gives me no ground for boasting. For necessity is laid upon me. Woe to me if I do not preach the Gospel!' (1 Cor 9:16). In the name of the whole Church, I sense an urgent duty to repeat this cry of St. Paul." Many Catholics take Jesus' command to go and make disciples of all nations as an instruction given to the apostles, to priests, and to religious, but not to them personally. Yet all of us are part of a plan of salvation much bigger than ourselves, and Jesus calls every Catholic to do his or her part in spreading the Gospel. There are many ways we can share our faith: through the gift of a book, a movie, an invitation to Mass, an invitation to the Rite of Christian Initiation of Adults (RCIA), by praying with someone, sharing a personal experience, mentioning a passage from Scripture, fasting and praying for others' conversions, and so on. Take a moment in silent prayer to ask, "Jesus, in what ways are you asking me to share my faith?"

THREE

PAPÁ JAIME

An open-hearted engineer descends into
the sewers of Bogotá, Colombia, to save street
children, and comes out a modern-day hero,
nominated for the Nobel Peace Prize.

At Christmastime in 1973, I was walking down the streets of
Bogotá, in my beloved home country of Colombia. After com-
pleting two master's degrees in inspection and exploration
in geophysics, first in Austria and then in Germany, I had returned to Colombia and begun working in the oil industry as a
physics and petroleum engineer.

That day, as I walked along, a Fisher Price toy box decorat-
ed with the picture of a doll suddenly fell onto the road from
a passing car. A group of street children noticed it and immediately ran into the street. A little girl reached it first, and with
a look of triumphant glee, lifted up the box above her head.
Her eyes met mine, and the expression on her face said clearly, "Look what I found!" Happy and radiant, she continued
to stare directly at me, smiling broadly, and I smiled back—
neither of us aware that a large truck was advancing toward
her at an alarming speed. The truck driver slammed on the

brakes, but it was already too late: the right side of his trailer crushed her against the pavement. Seized with sorrow, I stepped toward that heart-wrenching scene. Next to her dead body lay the toy box. It was empty.

That empty Fisher Price toy box was a divine sign for me. In that moment, I began to understand my mission in this world.

With all the grief, resentment, and anger that I felt, I went to a shopping center and purchased a Santa Claus costume. Then after lifting a sack of a hundred cheap presents onto my back, I walked out into the streets as Saint Nick to distribute the gifts to the children of the streets. I discovered that each of them lived in ghastly conditions, surrounded by the most extreme poverty; and as if that weren't enough, many of them had terrible physical defects that sank them even further into their miserable state.

Seeing me, a little boy ran forward and said, "Hey, are you Santa Claus?"

I said, "Yes."

"Wait a second," he said and whistled loudly. Suddenly, from I don't know where, more children showed up than I had presents for. The little boy grabbed me and jumped up on my back, he was so happy. Then I noticed that the sleeve of my costume had a yellowish mark on it. And then I noticed a stench.

I set the boy down on the ground and looked at him. My beard had scratched his face, and my sleeve had touched a large pus-filled hole where a rat had bitten his cheek so deeply as to damage his bone. I took him to the doctor and kept in touch with him, giving him attention, love, and support. I learned that his was not an isolated case.

Many of these children were burned, disabled, or otherwise wounded. So I came back many times to take more and more of them to hospitals for medical treatment, with the idea of eventually giving them the means to convert themselves into self-sufficient people. I also began to buy and disperse goods to the children: shiny shoes, tools for washing cars, old bicycles . . . Thus was born, on that Christmas in 1973, la Fundación Niños de los Andes (Foundation for the Children of the Andes), a foundation I still help run that rescues, raises, and rehabilitates street children.

After time passed, many of them went to work in the petroleum industry. That being my camp of professional activity, it was relatively easy for me to obtain work for them in the different areas of petroleum exploration. Today, the little boy who jumped on my back is an engineer who has helped more than one hundred street children by taking them under his own care.

Through the years, I've received various divine signs—hints of my true mission, each one clearer than the last, with the same elements and characters—that somehow inspired me to dream and to act.

I Became a Mischievous, Wild, and Curious Child —a Real Rebel Against Injustice

I came from a wealthy Catholic family in Manizales, Colombia, and grew up as the center of attention in a home full of affection. The first of three boys, I was born of a young couple married in the 1950s. My parents demonstrated their charity and love in many ways, especially by helping people on their farm and in their hardware store called Almacen El Pintor. My grandparents, too, gave of themselves to others lovingly and generously. In my wider family, four women became nuns. We were a family surrounded by faith, and I always believed in God, even as a small child. Although I resented being forced to go to Mass every day and to say the holy rosary, which at the time seemed endless to me, I learned to pray; and I came to believe that if you don't have faith, you are dead. The faith God gave me isn't the faith of St. Thomas, who said: "Unless I see and touch your wounds, I will not believe." I have always first believed, and then I see.

I became a mischievous, wild, and curious child—a real rebel against injustice—because I couldn't understand the beliefs that were separating human beings according to the money, the power, the prestige, or the reputation that they possessed. In Colombia, people fall into distinct classes, from the abject poor to the very wealthy. I made friends with people of many different classes, and it made no sense to me that I couldn't bring my friends to a country club. I especially couldn't comprehend why others less fortunate than I had to suffer so much. Fighting the system, I acted out, broke the rules, and got punished for it.

Once, when I was almost seven years old, I seriously asked myself why I felt I was a very naughty boy. I seemed so different from other children! My teachers tried, by all sorts of means, to make me just like the others. I went to a school run by strict Spanish nuns, and every morning the school bus picked me up from home. It was also supposed to take me back to my house in the afternoon, but I usually had to stay after school as a punishment. I could never understand why my parents paid for transportation in the afternoons, since I was never on that bus.

The nuns subjected me to myriad punishments for different reasons: for being fidgety; for making too much noise; for being disobedient; for not keeping my notebooks as required; for being undisciplined, laughing out loud, and getting dirty.

As a punishment, they sometimes made me run nonstop around the soccer field, not only during recess, but also after everyone else had gone home. The nuns kept me after school to learn the multiplication tables, not like other children did, from the numbers one to nine, but from eleven to ninety-nine. If I made one mistake, I had to stay at least another half-hour repeating them.

They told me to sit in a pine tree forest alone, in silence, not moving for long periods of time, depending on the fault for which I was accused; and sometimes, the nuns put me to work in poor neighborhoods with the missionaries. Those punishments I didn't mind.

Other times, they sent me to a corner in the classroom where I had to sit down in front of a white poster that said, "I am stupid," or "I am an idiot who doesn't understand anything," while the other kids laughed at me. One day, I took the idiot of the town to school, brought him to the classroom, and sat him in my corner. When the nun tried to get him out, he got furious and violent. Scared to death, she begged me to take him out. From that day on, I was never punished again like that.

My worst punishment came for being left-handed: they told me I was the son of the devil and that the "Bogey Man" would take me at night if I didn't start writing with my right hand. So that I would overcome my left-handedness, they hit my left hand with a ruler and made me write thousands of sentences with my right hand on the blackboard, such as: "I am a very good, loving, patient, peaceful, and helpful child." While all the other children went happily home, Mother Superior would sometimes take me to the schoolyard and force me to stand in front of a huge dog named Leal, whom the sisters had tied up with a chain. I can still hear Leal's bark, see his piercing eyes and his menacing jaws. I ended up with the dog so frequently that I began bringing him food. Soon we became friends.

One afternoon, while I watched the children play from the corner in the yard, I decided to let the dog loose. I untied his chain, and he ran directly toward the nun who punished me the most, bit her in her rear, and then went after another nun who was running for her life. He bit her, too, but I don't know where. I just know she had to be taken to the hospital. In the middle of the confusion, my school friends and I snuck into the cloister, forbidden territory for the students. There we found a pantry full of fruits, cookies, cakes, and consecration wine. We left with our loot and distributed it among the families in the neighborhood who lived in conditions unfit for human beings.

The contrast between the wealth and comfort of my school and the misery and hopelessness of those children who lived just a few streets away caught my attention. I remember the delight of my schoolmates as they saw how those children gobbled up the food we had given them. Innocently the children asked us when we would return. We visited those boys and girls again, and they filled my childhood with love and happiness, giving meaning to my life and to that of some of my schoolmates. God was giving me my first sign of what my mission in this world would be.

I Learned That I Was Happier Giving Than Receiving

More signs followed as my spirit felt inspired to navigate the divide between the rich and the poor. One day, at age eight, as I was coming home from school after a dreadful downpour, I found an old man with a boy in front of my house. The boy, who looked my age, was shivering from cold and hunger. When the old man saw me, he asked me for a coin or for something to eat. I said, "Don't go away. I'll be back in five minutes." I ran to my house, climbed the stairs, and got into my mother's closet; I pulled out two blankets, a few towels, and some shirts, pants, and shoes that my father didn't use. Then I went into my closet and did the same thing. From the cupboard in the kitchen, I got some milk, eggs, soups, tomatoes, and chocolate bars. I wrapped all of the stuff up in the blankets and hurried back, fearing that the old man and the boy might have left. But they had stayed there waiting for me. That moment remains one of the happiest of my childhood. My heart brimmed with joy, and my breath was short.

That night, I still felt so happy about what I had done. But Estercita, our longtime nanny, had seen me get the stuff together and told my parents what had happened. They got very angry because I had given all those things away without permission, so I was scolded and punished. I couldn't understand why and asked them, "If you have so many clothes and so much food put away, why can't I give some of it away? Isn't there enough for all of us?" But my words only made them angrier. Then, sad and crying, I packed my small gray bag with cocoa, powdered milk, some chocolate bars, my notebooks, my short pants and suspenders, a shirt, a little car, and a small image of the Virgin of Fatima that glowed in the dark. I looked steadily at my parents and told them in a defying tone, "You are hycropites." I may have pronounced "hypocrites" incorrectly, but I knew what it meant, and I knew it was rude. I announced that I was leaving and walked out the front door in great disappointment. After circling the block several times, I decided to go and live with my grandmother.

As it got dark, my parents found out where I had gone and came to fetch me. They asked me to come back with them, but

I didn't want to return under any circumstance. I emphatically reminded them that when my mother visited the old folks' home, she was allowed to take them blankets, clothes, and even cigarettes, which I knew gave them bad breath and bad teeth. Finally, my mother hugged me, and smiling, said to me sweetly, "Honey, I understand how you feel in your generous heart. It is so big that it made you leave your parents, who love you very much. But if you leave us to help others, you will be a light in the street; but there will be darkness in our home." We negotiated an agreement, and I went back home.

When my parents punished me for helping the old man and the boy, I knew I had two options. I could obey my heart, that inner voice or divine spark, that never fails; or I could listen to my parents, who, in fear, tried to teach me a lesson in order to prevent me from making my own decisions without their consent. Since I chose the first, I learned that I was happier giving than receiving, and that when I gave without expecting a reward, my heart could soar upward with joy and unite with God who is inside one's heart.

During my school vacations, my family and I would go to my parents' farm, and my greatest pleasure was riding my horse, alongside my dog, to the coffee plantations on the top of the mountain. The foreman lived up there with his children: a girl age eight, like I was, and her younger brother. I always stopped by to have a cup of delicious agua de panela with lemon (a Colombian hot beverage made with sugar cane). On one of those occasions, I saw that the foreman's daughter was playing with a plastic doll that was missing a foot and a hand—a horrid toy. This shocked me completely, all the more so when I saw her little brother playing with a shattered wooden truck without wheels. When I got home, I asked my father why those children didn't have any new, good toys, like we did. Didn't their father work, too?

My father took me over to the coffee greenhouse and told me, "Son, while we are on vacation, fill these little bags with black earth; and with a lot of patience, plant one seed in every bag. I'll give you one cent for each one you make, and with that money you will be able to buy a doll and a good truck for the foreman's children." No sooner said than done. I worked and worked, planting coffee beans. I also asked my brothers, my friends, and other relatives to help me with the job.

Finally, the great day arrived when my father came to see what we had done. We counted the bags, and with the money I had earned, we went to buy a spectacular doll and a huge wooden truck. The next day, I got up very early and swiftly rode over to the foreman's house to give the children their presents. I felt incredibly happy, and when I got off the horse, I said to the girl, "Look what I brought you. This is for you." The girl stared at me blankly. Then she looked at the doll with misgivings and suspicion and would not take it. She probably thought I was lending it to her and would ask for it back later on. Meanwhile, her little brother came over to look at the truck and asked me if it was for him. I hadn't finished answering when he climbed up into it and started riding downhill. At last, the girl shyly picked up the doll and smiled happily. I felt close to her at that moment and have ever since. It was then, in that accomplishment, that I experienced for the first time in my life the presence of God as love.

The next year, during one of our fourth grade class mission projects—led by Brother Cardona—I found out that Néstor, the night watchman at school, lived in a cold, ugly, foul, and miserable room. I decided to sell my miniscuí (fruit salts with sugar and food coloring wrapped up in a paper cone). With the money I received, I planned to build a house for the watch-man. For my project, my father donated paint and building materials from the hardware store he owned. With his aid, the help of my fellow scouts, as well as the extremely helpful work of a humble, enthusiastic priest whom we called "Bu-ñuelo" Gutiérrez, we secured a vacant lot and began build-ing on the weekends. After several months, we managed to finish the house—the result of the love and work of a team of children who shared the same dream. Later, it became part of a complete neighborhood called San Luis Gonzaga, with seventy-two homes.

I Dreamed of Rescuing All These Children

God had prepared me for the December day in 1973 when I would see the little girl lying lifeless in the street next to an empty toy box. Little did I know that God was going to give me another life-changing sign. Ten years later, while I was driving to the oil company where I worked as a petroleum en-gineer, I entered into a big traffic jam. "What's going on?" I wondered. I stepped out of my car and followed a crowd of people onto a bridge to see what was happening; and again, I found another little girl, lying on the ground. She was writhing in pain, thrashing and flailing about. Out of her mouth came white foam, and blood covered her body. I remembered the first little girl who lost her life in the street, and recognized that God was again calling me to act.

As I approached the scene, I heard bystanders saying that a car had run over her. "I'll take her to a hospital," I said.

But the others warned me, "Don't take her. If you take her to the hospital and she dies, you'll end up in prison."

"I don't care," I answered, and I picked up the girl, placed her in my car, and took her to the county clinic. I waited for a while. Then to my surprise, after she received the necessary medical attention, she walked out with the doctor. He explained that she hadn't been run over by a car, but had suffered an attack of epilepsy and must have struck her head against the sidewalk. Surprised and overjoyed to see her well, I hugged her and asked her, "So tell me, sweetheart, where do you live?" I wanted to return her to the comfort of her home and parents as soon as possible.

Shyly, she told me, "I don't have any parents, and I live in the sewer by the bridge where you picked me up." I had never before heard about children living in the sewers below the city streets.

"Come, then," I said, hiding my astonishment. "Show me where you live."

Dressed in a suit and tie, both of them stained with blood, I entered the sewer behind her, and what I experienced reminded me of the hell that Dante described in *The Divine Comedy*. The view was terrifying. The ground was slick with filth, and the odor of human excrement asphyxiating. We entered deeper and deeper, little by little, into this fearful, dark landscape, full of sadness and chilling cold. The air grew more dense, with a strange warmth penetrating the fetid atmosphere. As we walked, I sensed rats and cockroaches darting and scurrying, from one side to another, in the frigid water covering our feet.

Suddenly the darkness was complete. At that moment, I thought of turning around and saying to her, "Well, little one, now I've seen what it's like, and this is as far as I'm going to go." But I had to continue. I couldn't tell her no, even though the freezing, foul-smelling water reached up to my knees and my legs were growing numb.

Then the girl lit a small candle she was carrying, providing a dim, flickering light, which offered almost no visibility. We continued advancing. She pointed to some boards several feet ahead that bridged a black stream. On the other side, I could see a bunch of old rags and wet newspapers. After crossing the boards, I tripped over something on the ground. I looked down to see the outline of a television set, perhaps stolen. Next to the television stood a table. On top of the table lay a "bed," or what is called, in that underworld, a *cambuche*: a plank or shelf, about head-high, topped with sacks and blankets. There, above the pipes and streams of black, foul waters, amidst an unbearable stench, my little friend and her ten companions had formed their nest. I couldn't believe my eyes.

In that horrid place where night seemed eternal and despair and fear reigned, my body froze, my heart shrunk, and my mind stopped working. But my spirit felt enlightened, brimming over with faith, passion, and love, as I visualized a dream of rescuing, one by one, all those children of the darkness in my beloved Colombia. That day I learned that these and thousands of other children lived in the nooks and crannies of the sewers of Bogotá, which rest on top of an ancient Roman-style sewage system with wide open tunnels and caves. The children's survival depends upon whether or not they can keep their heads above the human waste, for when it's raining, the sewage rises up and washes away everything in its path.

The little girl began to introduce me to her gang. Longing to remove them from this place of complete darkness, I said to them, "So why don't we go to a restaurant to eat something? Come out of here. I will take you." When we entered into the light of day, I saw that one of the children, a small boy, had a cleft palate and harelip, which disfigured his face terribly. "Come with me," I said to him. "I know a very good doctor who can do a surgery for you."

As soon as I spoke, the other kids got very angry and said, "No, no, no. You cannot take him."

"Why not?" I asked. A confused dialogue ensued, and at some point in the midst of it, I understood their protest. The boy was how they survived. He begged so that they could live.

To Love Without Limits

From that moment forward, I resolved that I would search out all the other hidden crevices in that dark, underground world, and I would remove all the children that lived there, one by one.

I started telling my dream to everyone I met. Some people helped me, others mocked me, while still others told me that I was out of my mind. I had two options. One was to heed the murderers of dreams, who criticized and doubted me, treating me like a fool, telling me to draw limits to my dreams, assuring me that my goal was impossible to reach. They said it was a problem that should be solved by the government, that there were too many children in the sewers, and I could not possibly rescue them all. They said it was too dangerous, that I could be attacked or get sick with typhus fever, hepatitis, or leprosy. But the other option was to listen to my inner voice and to my heart; to love without limits what I proposed to do; to act with passion, perseverance, and courage, despite the opposition of the majority.

The sewers posed many dangers—the threat of infectious disease, freezing-cold temperatures, slippery surfaces, and noxious fumes. Water pipes were known to break, and torrents of sewage water would rush through, destroying everything in their path—sometimes sweeping away the children and drowning them. The children knew that when the rains came, they were in danger. They also knew that the rats were un-afraid to bite, and always aimed for the eyes, nose, mouth, or genitals. So as the children slept, they kept candles lit nearby to stave off the insidious intruders. And if a human intruder entered their territory, the children could jump the person, fearing for their lives. I was not entering welcoming surroundings. What could I do?

One day, while I was scuba diving off the island of Providence, an inspiration came to me. I had heard of a cave of incredible beauty at the bottom of the sea and felt a strong desire to see it. Traveling behind a guide, I entered the cave's interior, and as a virtual underwater paradise surrounded me, I visualized those dark passages in Bogotá, and I said to myself, "Here's the solution." I returned to Bogotá and entered into the sewers with the same scuba diving equipment, and thus began to roam the dark tunnels with my rubber wet suit, tank, regulator, and mask.

The scuba gear offered many advantages: I avoided the nauseating odors and didn't have to breathe that rare, toxic mix of air, gas, and excrement; and the suit protected me partially from the cold. Not only that, the equipment included a powerful diving light to guide my way. The initial tank I used proved too heavy, but later I exchanged it for a smaller, more manageable one. All of this facilitated my rescue work, and no longer did I feel the need to exit rapidly due to lack of oxygen, nor was I threatened by poisonous intoxication.

During one of my nighttime underground visits, an incident occurred that we still laugh about at the foundation. At the same time that a drug addict was smoking crack cocaine underneath a bridge, at the entrance to a sewage pipe, I was walking out of the sewers in my formidable scuba gear. Around my neck, I carried a large medical kit, stamped with a large Red Cross symbol, in which I stored disinfectant, acupuncture needles, and antibiotics; and strapped to my body was my oxygen regulator that made a formidable sound in the sewer—a rapid, repetitive ussssh . . . USSSSH . . . so the sound of my breathing mimicked that of Darth Vader. And if that weren't strange enough, I also carried my powerful diving light in hand.

When the young man saw that large Red Cross symbol illuminated by my searchlight, and cables cascading from my black face mask, he received the fright of his life and started shouting, "Satan! Satan! Don't take me!" My heart almost exploded. For a split second, I wondered if the devil had just made a personal appearance. But as soon as I caught sight of the young man, he ran away from me like a bullet, disappearing across the slick and slippery pavement. I doubt he ever smoked again. I figure that was the most successful drug rehabilitation case we've had.

I Saw the Death Squads Kill Children

The children in the sewers and on the streets suffer in a living hell. They pass through endless nights, looking for someone to take care of them or just offer them a kind word. They don't know what it is like to play. They don't know what it is to feel joy. Abandoned, without a mother or father, thrown into corruption, drug addiction, and violence, they live in constant despair. They have to steal to survive, and they use drugs in order to steal, in a hopeless attempt to combat their abject misery.

As if their state of existence wasn't punishment enough, fearsome death squads began to form in Colombia—secret organizations made up of corrupt, crazy, insensible people, and guns for hire, who were bent on exterminating the children. They fashioned a "social cleansing" plan. These squads felt that young indigents, beggars, and petty thieves of the street no longer had the capacity for rehabilitation, and that it was better to kill them while they were still children, before they became worse criminals. Besides, it was easier and cheaper to kill them than help them, so they began "cleaning" away the disposable children from the streets, dens, sewers, pipes, and bridges. Shop owners and other victims of the children's crimes encouraged the death squads, paying them to kill certain children whom they had come to hate.

I watched corrupt policemen take a young street girl, douse her with gasoline, and light her on fire in the middle of the street, leaving her to die. She had stolen from a store merchant, and the police were making her an example for the others of their new extermination policy. Even more heartless was the reaction of the people nearby. They simply ignored her, walking over and around her. Horrified, I took her to a nearby hospital for treatment.

It is unthinkable what the death squads have done to the children, even to little girls, whom they have raped and tortured. Many times I saw the death squads kill the children. The most terrible thing I ever witnessed happened in 1985, when I saw a death squad pouring gasoline into a street drain, onto a large group of children who were just below in a drain hole. The squad lit them on fire, then left them for dead. I rushed underground to where they were, and what I saw was grotesque. The children were still alive. They were screaming and crying as their skin was burning off of them. Their arms and legs looked charred, and their flesh was peeling away from their faces. I put them in the car and took them to the hospital. The pain they endured had no words or measure.

I may have helped those few children, but the death squads continued to open manholes in the street and pour gasoline down them, killing many children, again and again.

One day when I was in my thirties, as I was climbing through the hills of Colombia, I felt very disappointed with God and asked him, "Why are they killing so many street children? They set them on fire. They torture them. The children are human beings, already in their greatest state of degradation, dealing with depression and suicide, and you don't do anything!" At that time, the police were against me. My wife was worried about my well-being—especially now that we were raising two children—and she worried about the drain on our earnings as I poured them into the foundation. People were condemning and criticizing me. Jealousy and false rumors were growing, trying to destroy the work that was God's and not mine. I was also under great stress because the death squads were making real threats against my life. Twice now, I had been kidnapped by gangs who preyed on the affluent for ransoms, and they let me go unharmed only because they found out who I was and the work I was doing.

In the middle of my desperation, confusion, and sadness over feeling so alone, hurt, and abandoned, I cried out to the Almighty: "My God, why have you abandoned me? Why have you left me alone? Why do you let them treat me like this?" An entire evening passed as I asked God where he had gone. "Appear!" I said to him. "Show yourself to me! Defend me!"

That night I entered a restaurant and asked to use the telephone. When I hung up the receiver, I looked up and saw a poster with a picture of footprints imprinted on a sandy beach.

Underneath it was the well-known poem "Footprints in the Sand," which I had never seen before. It tells of a person who dreams he is walking along the beach, accompanied by God. During the walk, many scenes from his life flash across the sky, while at the same time, one or two sets of footprints form in the sand. He grows worried, noticing that during the sad scenes of his life, when he had to endure the greatest suffering, only one set of footprints is there. The man asks God why he wasn't walking beside him during the difficult times, even though God had promised he'd always be there. And the Lord tells him that the times the man saw only one set of footprints were when God was carrying him in his arms.

As I stared at the poem, my eyes couldn't at first take in what I was reading. Then upon truly digesting the poem's message, my life and my attitude changed. I left completely happy, feeling that marvelous interior calm that we can only encounter when we are at peace with God and with ourselves. This helped me continue on.

Around 1990, my work with the children of the sewers was featured on the TV show *20/20*. I felt it was important that people knew in what conditions the children lived. The ABC crew followed me into the sewers and saw some of the boys and girls lying prostrate, seemingly asleep. As we walked by, they asked, "Why don't they wake up?"

I said, "Because they are dead."

The crew didn't believe me. When they realized what I said was true, they cried and cried, and they could not film that day. I have never seen people cry as much as they did. Because of *20/20* coverage, the death squads were halted, and a lot of the corrupt policemen who were part of the squads were fired.

God Prepared Me Well for the Many Losses I Would Encounter in Life

The death squads killed many of the children I had come to know and love, and I had to pass many times through the fire of loss. No death, however, has ever been as hard for me as was my first encounter with it when I was a child and my beloved grandmother Maria died.

As one of my grandmother's favorite grandchildren, I was often by her side. When she became ill, she asked for me constantly. My parents worried that her death would be an extremely difficult experience for me; they thought I might not be able to overcome it, since I was so close to her. Finally the day came when she left this world. When I heard the heartbreaking news, I cried as never before or since.

As time passed, I understood that although my grandmother would never again be in this world, she would always be in my heart, and she would be the light of my life in troublesome times. God prepared me well for the many losses I would encounter in life.

I Realized I Would Have to Let Go

One terrible loss for me to accept occurred underground one night in 1991, in the dark, infernal passageways of the sewers. Earlier that day, I had met a man from the United States named Wayne Weible, who writes and speaks about something I had never heard of before then—that Our Lady was appearing in Medjugorje. He asked me if I could take him into the sewers to see the children.

I told him that the sewers were dangerous; that the children, many of whom were taking drugs, could consider him a threat. He persisted, telling me he thought that Our Lady wanted him to accompany me.

I warned him that he could become very ill, and told him how members of the crew of *20/20* had to be hospitalized after entering the sewers. I told him of how the children needed to keep candles by their sides while they slept so the rats wouldn't bite. He seemed undeterred, so I left for the sewers to prepare the children for Wayne's coming, in order to make the journey safe for him.

That evening, as I entered the sewers, I found a brother and a sister, ages five and seven. I told them I would take them to the foundation, and as I was bringing them out, one of the bigger pipes, clogged with debris and waste, suddenly broke. I grabbed the children, holding one in each arm, as torrents of sewage water passed between my legs and around us, with such a force that I could barely withstand it. The water seemed intent on destroying everything in its path, and the children were crying and screaming, "Hold me! Hold me! Don't let me go!" I held on to them with every bit of strength I had. It was terrible. The water was relentless, and after a while my arms grew tired.

Eventually, I realized I would have to let go of one of the children. I didn't want to have to choose. I was forced into a nightmare of having to "kill" a child. I said to myself, "The one who isn't strong enough to hold onto me, and whom I can no longer hold onto, will go." A hernia had developed in my abdomen, and my hip joint was tearing.

My strength was fading. In agony, I let go of the boy, and he was swept away and drowned in the sewage water.

My mind usually blocks out that event. I find it too painful to remember. After it happened, I needed thirty minutes outside to recollect myself, and then I went back into the sewers to look for more children who might have been hurt. Then I took the little girl to the foundation and got her settled.

"It's Papá Jaime!"

I was supposed to pick up Wayne at 11:00 p.m. It was now 5:00 a.m., on a cold and rainy morning. I had been in the sewers all night. I called Wayne and asked him if he still wanted to go. He said yes.

I picked him up at his hotel, and we took off, flying through the streets of Bogotá. After a few minutes, Wayne said, "Jaime, you're running all these red lights."

I told him, "We don't stop on the streets here. It's not safe—not even to stop at a red light. You have to keep moving." Then we stopped at an outdoor market café, offering an assortment of sandwiches, breads, and drinks. I handed the clerk two large sacks and asked him to fill them with food. Standing at the entrance of the door, peering in hungrily, stood an older man, thin as a rail, in rags, freezing and thoroughly soaked. I motioned for him to come into the store, and told the clerk to give him anything he asked for. The man hurried to the counter, ignoring the disdainful look of the clerk and bystanders in the café.

Then an emaciated little boy, living on the streets, seeing what had happened, came up to me and asked if he, too, could have something to eat. I jostled his long, wet hair and said to the clerk, "Give him whatever he wants." Reluctantly, the clerk gave them food; they both were so grateful, they helped us load everything into the car. Thousands in Colombia, such as they, receive no aid and beg to survive.

As I drove the car away, I could see them in my rear-view mirror yelling, "Thank you! Thank you!"

Daylight was breaking, and it was still raining when we arrived at the entrance to the sewers. With Wayne following me, we waded into the putrid water soaring out of a large drainpipe. I turned on my flashlight and started shouting, "It's Papá Jaime! It's Papá Jaime! Come here! It's Papá Jaime!" Children of all ages and sizes began emerging out of little cracks and crevices, none of them smiling, just looking around hesitantly, until they came close enough to see me. Then a slight smile appeared on some of their faces.

The food I brought was a feast for them. They didn't rush the bags; they didn't tear at them. They very patiently waited as I passed out the food, which took quite some time. Wayne looked crushed by what he saw. I decided to escort eight of the children out of the tunnel. I felt they needed to come to the foundation right away. Several others followed, asking me if they could take more food to other children hidden within the maze of pipes; I gave it to them, knowing they would hand the food to those who were sick or hiding. They have a code of honor amongst themselves, no matter what they may have done.

The ten of us piled into my small car and took off toward the foundation center; but first, I wanted to make another stop to check on a girl and her baby. I pulled up under an overpass and onto a muddy field, stopping near the entrance to another drainpipe, where seven or eight children approached me. I had one bag of food left. Suddenly, a police van arrived. Wayne was wondering if this was because there were too many people in the car. The van parked next to us, and several policemen got out and began walking toward me. They knew who I was, and what I was doing. They told me they were going to take the children and Wayne to the police station. They wanted to investigate why a foreigner was with us.

I tried to talk them out of taking everyone away to the station, but several policemen began herding the children into the van. Following in close pursuit, I again tried to bargain with them. I told them that the children wouldn't cause trouble anymore. I told them that Wayne was a great asset to the foundation, even though this argument meant almost nothing to them. Twenty tension-filled minutes passed as I tried to negotiate an agreement. Miraculously, they let us go, and some of the officers even helped me get my car out of the mud and onto the road so we could leave. Wayne, who was unaware of what our heated words in Spanish had meant, exclaimed: "It was Our Lady who protected us!"

I Wanted to Go to Medjugorje to Express My Thankfulness

I didn't tell Wayne what had actually transpired with the police that morning until two years later. He was grateful for the delay. Wayne later told me that not only had Our Lady inspired him to go into the sewers but also to begin a special project called Children of the Sewers—an effort to raise awareness and funds for the Fundacion Niños de los Andes.

From that moment, the Virgin of Medjugorje became the patroness of the foundation. I am confident that she is keeping an eye on all the boys and girls as they go forward in life, and I have always relied on her to help keep us afloat. God, who is my helper, has multiple ways of coming to our aid, and one of his most beautiful ways is through Our Lady, who for me, represents love, compassion, and mercy.

In 2005, as with many other times, we were in a big financial hole. We were overdrafting, unable to pay for medical bills, food, and the paychecks for our staff. To continue, we needed

$58,000 immediately. The bank said, "Sorry, no money. And we can't offer you any kind of overdraft."

And I said, "Okay, let's see what happens."

Then an hour later, Wayne Weible called me from the United States and said, "Jaime, I've got some money for you."

Just moments prior, Wayne Weible's secretary had told him, "Sit down," and then proceeded to show him a heartfelt letter in support of our work with the Children of the Sewers, along with a signed check for $51,000. Then, between the time Wayne called me and the moment he went to deposit the check, he had received another $7,000. So I received $58,000, the exact amount we needed.

In addition to alerting me to donations from the United States, Wayne, for ten years following the day we met, also persisted in trying to get me to go on a pilgrimage with him to Medjugorje; but for one reason or another, with my relentlessly busy calendar, I was never able to go.

In November 2005, my schedule did finally open up, giving me the chance to travel to this special place. I wanted to go to Medjugorje to express my thankfulness to Our Lady, because to me, she is like a wonderful mama, always there, always helping the foundation whenever we have problems.

I literally had to escape from my work in order to go. For the ten days I was away, I kept up with communications over the Internet, but no one knew where I was. Arrangements happened at the last minute—my visa, plane tickets, et cetera—so I ended up flying out of Colombia a day late, and I almost didn't make it. When I passed through Washington, D.C., and went to the embassy there in order to get another visa to allow me into Bosnia and Herzegovina, the clerk said I would have to come back the next day at four in the afternoon to receive it.

I thought to myself, "Well, I have so much to do at home. I'm not going to be able to go. I'll just return to Colombia." Persevering, nevertheless, I told the man behind the counter, "No. I'll wait here for the visa," and then I sat down. He handed me the visa within an hour.

After I arrived in Medjugorje, I kept with my tradition of meditating in nature, which I have done for thirty-seven years. These are magical and sacred moments for me in which I connect with God, with thanksgiving and appreciation for all the beautiful things he has done for me.

Every day in Medjugorje, I woke up at four in the morning to climb Cross Mountain. One day something strange happened. When I arrived at the top of the mountain, I was very convinced, full of faith, that the Virgin was going to appear to me, just as she does to the visionaries. Then I felt the strong presence of a beautiful, divine energy, a healing energy, and I sensed that Our Lady was there. She seemed so close that I said to her, "Hey, why don't you show yourself to me, as you do to the visionaries? Please, let me see you." I was completely open to whatever might happen. "Come on! Come on!" I urged. "Other people see you. Why can't I?" But she didn't show up.

Another morning, I again climbed Cross Mountain in the cold morning air. Near the white stone cross placed at the summit, I sat down to meditate and drifted into a dreamlike state. In that moment of peace, interior harmony, and love, I saw an image, or perhaps a vision, in which the Virgin of Medjugorje came toward me and told me that many people pray just to pray, but aren't conscious of how they think, or what they say, or how they act, and upon finishing their prayers, forget the loving motive of giving to others the best that is in their hearts, without expecting anything in return.

After receiving this beautiful message, I sat to reflect on the words of the Virgin—with which I wholeheartedly agreed. As a result, in that sublime moment, she inspired me to propose to those I would meet along life's way that every time they prayed the Our Father, they should do so conscientiously, feeling the beauty and wisdom in its words and applying them each day, rather than simply repeating them automatically.

For in our humanness, we say, "Our Father, who art in heaven," and many times we don't appreciate him or behave like his children.

We say, "Hallowed be thy name," and with any problem or blow that strikes us, we curse in his name and blame him for it.

We say, "Thy kingdom come. Thy will be done, on earth as it is in heaven," when what we love isn't the kingdom of the spiritual realm, but the kingdom of power, ego, competition, and avarice—the insatiable desire to have and to amass.

We say, "Give us this day our daily bread," but when we have the opportunity to give or share with those who are hungry, we choose not to feed them.

We say, "And forgive us our trespasses, as we forgive those who trespass against us," but we act like Pharisees because we say that we forgive others, but we don't know that to forgive is to remember without pain, without resentment.

We say, "Lead us not into temptation," but since God has given us free will, we seek ways to fall into temptation in order to satisfy our desires, which come from our egos.

We say, "But deliver us from evil," but we judge, we criticize, and we cause harm to others; or we turn a blind eye to the face of injustice, doing nothing—and, like parrots, we say, "Amen," without realizing what we have just promised.

I awoke from this vision, this dream, startled to see a tall man standing over me, lifting up prayers in a very loud voice, with his hands placed on my head. Astonished, I wondered, "Did I die? What's happening to me?" The man stepped back and began to walk down the mountain. I pulled out my camera, hoping to catch the presence of Our Lady, taking pictures of the area where I thought I had seen her; and then I got up and followed the man, trying to take a picture of him, because I didn't know if he was real or an angel. At five in the morning, in the middle of winter, in that penetrating cold on top of the mountain, I had never imagined encountering anyone.

Love Is for Giving

I am Catholic, but I am completely convinced that prayer, meditation, or contemplation without action, without service to others, is incomplete. I remember Mother Teresa of Calcutta telling me, after we shared an International Peace Award and became very good friends, "Papá Jaime, power is for service; love is for giving; and prayer without action and without service to others is worthless." She also said that it means nothing if I pray beautifully, if I recite a million rosaries, and then leave my home and step over someone who is hungry, or ignore someone who is thirsty, or see someone with a problem and don't help him.

God gives us signs, calling us to help others all the time, but we may not notice them. One morning at sunrise, after my usual time of meditation, as I was climbing down the Guadalupe Mountain in Bogotá, returning to the city to begin my tasks, a couple of burglars surprised me. The oldest one yelled excitedly while holding a knife that trembled at the rhythm of his heart: "This is a holdup."

I stared at him and said, "I know this is a holdup, but put down that knife before you gouge out one of your eyes." Then calmly, I added, "As you can see, I have no valuables with me, but if there is anything you need, I will be very glad to help you."

Immediately, anxiety vanished from his face. When he recognized me, deeply moved and sobbing, he said, "Look, Papá Jaime, I am not a robber, nor a thief, and this boy you see here is my son, whom I have taught to be honest, to respect and serve others, and to have good manners. But, what's happening is that my daughter is seriously ill. She is at the hospital, but they will not treat her unless we pay for the medicines. I used to work for the Bogotá Telephone Company (Telecom), but they fired me, and I don't have any health insurance to cover the medical expenses. That is why we came here to rob. If I don't do this, I won't be able to save my daughter."

I went to the hospital with them and told the doctors what was happening. They operated on the young girl and gave her free medical attention. How often we are wrong when we judge based on appearances and false beliefs, unable to see what lies behind a person's actions. We are not here to judge humanity, but to love it.

When people ask me about all the problems we have in Colombia—the drugs, the killing, the stealing—and they ask me how I feel about it, I tell them these things don't affect or concern me much. The people who commit these bad acts are only 2 percent of the population. Rather than these thoughtless ones, who are doing harm to others, what concerns me are the other 98 percent, the "good" and indifferent people who are watching in silence and doing nothing.

Many people have a lot of money, a lot to give, and they don't do anything for others. That is hard for me to understand, especially when I see children on the streets and in the sewers. I'm not talking just about millionaires. I am speaking of people in general. Anyone can give attention, love, and compassion.

"I Cry for the Opportunities That I've Wasted and Not Helped Others"

I am on a daily television program called *Muy Buenos Días* (*A Very Good Morning*), and during one live broadcast, the host of the show, named Jota Mario, told me that someone had called the program to say that there was a little girl who was living with her ninety-three-year-old aunt in a slum, in subhuman conditions, and she needed a wheelchair. While on the air, I spoke about the case, and I talked about the importance of unconditional loving service and of giving without expecting anything to be given back to us. I remember saying, emphatically, that those things we don't use after one year no longer belong to us and should therefore be given to someone who needs them. I explained, clearly, that storerooms with old blankets, damaged pictures, unused bicycles, clothes, et cetera, should not even exist.

At the end of my part of the show, nearly one hundred people called me; ninety-nine of them told me that they also needed a wheelchair, and only one woman offered one that could be collected at her house. I told her that it might be a good idea for her to come to the television studio with the wheelchair so that we could give it, together, to the little girl who lived in a very poor neighborhood called Simon Bolivar. The woman answered by saying that she trusted me, and she had no problem having the chair picked up. I responded that it wasn't a question of trust, but rather of feeling the joy, satisfaction, and pleasure of being able to give something personally. After much encouragement, she agreed to come with me to the little girl's home in Hangman's Hill in Ciudad Bolivar, where people often hang themselves out of despair.

The sewage of Hangman's Hill slops along the surface of the ground and flows into a canal wedged on the slope. When she arrived there and sensed the cold and putrid environment, the woman wanted to turn back. But finally we came to a dark and dense room where this twelve-year-old creature lived. We were told that the budding breasts of the child were totally ruined by wounds and calluses because, for the greater part of her life, she had had to crawl like a snake to get about. As I picked her up, I was assaulted by a waft of foulness, worse than in the sewers.

We sat her on the wheelchair and took her out for a ride. When the girl got out in the sunlight and saw the mountains, she began to laugh in a loud and strange way. For a moment, I thought that she might be retarded, but she reacted this way because she had never been outside her room. She had never even seen a bus. We continued our outing until we got to the corner, where we stopped to try some food that was being grilled and sold in the street.

While we were eating, the woman cried and cried. I asked her why she was crying, and she answered, "Papá Jaime, you have no idea." I told her she should be happy to have done such a good deed for the unfortunate girl.

She looked at me, and with a tearful voice, said, "I am crying because I had that wheelchair in the garage at home for over eight years. I cry just thinking about this poor child, crawling like a snake on the ground, while all this time the chair was rusting from lack of use at home. She had never had an outing until today. I cry for the opportunities that I've wasted and not helped others."

In a never-ending urge to accumulate and to possess things, we can create in our homes or storage sites a humid and disagreeable place to deposit everything we don't need, selfishly thinking about the day when it will come in handy. And so we lose the opportunity of helping a human being who could desperately need these things we hoarded away—things slowly becoming useless and deteriorated.

It Is More Blessed to Give

When I was in Medjugorje, kneeling and praying the rosary in St. James Church, a little girl about one and a half years old came up to me and grabbed my rosary. Her mom interjected, "Hey, no!" But I let the girl have the rosary, and she gave me hers, a little plastic one.

Shortly after that I gave a talk for pilgrims, and a lady who attended gave me a large, beautiful, silver and gold rosary, handmade by her, which cost a fair amount. I took this as a sign from God. I could have said to the little girl, "Hey, give that back to me!" But when I give things without expecting anything in return, I receive so much more spiritually.

Signs from God occur all around us, asking us to take notice, asking us to change and to act. When the young street girl died for an empty Fisher Price toy box, I realized God was showing me my mission in life. That moment spurred the beginning of the Foundation for the Children of the Andes. Then God showed me another pivotal sign, the epileptic girl, convulsing in the street—a sign that led me to discover children living underground amidst human waste.

Today I go into the sewers whenever I can. I am the only person who goes below ground to help the children. It is a dangerous venture, so I don't allow others to do that job. If someone were to fall and drink the sewage, or if a rat were to bite and infect them, or if the fumes made them sick, or if the water level were to rise suddenly, that person could die. Not only that, the children, often taking drugs to mentally escape their situation, might fear that an intruder is a member of a death squad and jump that person.

When I patrol the streets in a rescue effort, I pass through dire poverty and hopelessness; when I descend underground, I enter into a surrealistic place of sickening darkness and endless nights, where children still wait to be rescued. There I see no love, no light, no affection—only desperation as they search in vain for consolation, for hope, for a hug, for a word of kindness. Yet there I find joy; I find my calling. I never draw attention to the hellish conditions in which the children live, nor do I treat them with pity. I act as though their surroundings were completely normal. My focus is on how I can help them. What moves me is love, and love is what can heal them.

Once when I was rescuing children from a sewer in Bogotá, I came up to the surface with my clothes wet and foul, and some people came up to me to tell me that they wouldn't do that for a million pesos, and that they considered me a saint. I replied that I wasn't a saint, nor would I do it for a million pesos, but that I enjoyed doing it because I did not act out of fear but love. My work for the foundation has always been, and will always be, only as a volunteer. I don't receive any money from it. In 1990, I was nominated for the Nobel Peace Prize, but I preferred to be busy helping the children instead of filling out all that paperwork, so I decided not to enter my name.

When you love what you do and do what you love, you aren't working, but only enjoying the richness of life. Rescuing the children is not a sacrifice for me. Nor does it imply any kind of suffering to find myself inside a sewer, surrounded by death and loneliness, because the sight of a boy or a girl with a full belly and a happy heart, with eyes filled with hope and faith, is a gift that gives me the greatest joy. My spirit, which feeds on service, can rejoice and vibrate with peace and happiness.

Dear children! Today I come to you with a motherly desire for you to give me your hearts. My children, do this with complete trust and without fear. In your hearts, I will put my Son and His mercy. Then, my children, you will look at the world around you with different eyes. You will see your neighbor. You will feel his pain and suffering. You will not turn your head away from those who suffer, because my Son turns His head away from those who do so. Children, do not hesitate.

—Mary's message of May 2, 2007, from www.Medjugorje.ws

FOR PRAYERFUL REFLECTION

While others made excuses about why helping the less fortunate is too difficult, unneeded, or undeserved, Jaime Jaramillo, even as a small child, raced to fix the problems of poverty and neglect. Little did he know that he was racing to serve the Lord himself.

When the Son of Man comes in his glory, and all the angels with him, he will sit upon his glorious throne, and all the nations will be assembled before him. And he will separate them one from another, as a shepherd separates the sheep from the goats. He will place the sheep on his right and the goats on his left. Then the king will say to those on his right, "Come, you who are blessed by my Father.

91

Inherit the kingdom prepared for you from the foundation of the world. For I was hungry and you gave me food, I was thirsty and you gave me drink, a stranger and you welcomed me, naked and you clothed me, ill and you cared for me, in prison and you visited me."

Then the righteous will answer him and say, "Lord, when did we see you hungry and feed you, or thirsty and give you drink? When did we see you a stranger and welcome you, or naked and clothe you? When did we see you ill or in prison, and visit you?" And the king will say to them in reply, "Amen, I say to you, whatever you did for one of these least brothers of mine, you did for me."

—Matthew 25:31–40

1. Did you possess a holy trait as a child that you see manifesting itself in your life today? Is there an aspect of your childhood personality that you've since lost and would like to get back? If so, ask Mother Mary to pray for you, that this trait may blossom in your life.

2. Jaime felt that the little girl who died in pursuit of an empty Fisher Price toy box was a divine sign from God that he should act. Has something happened in your life that you sensed, upon prayerful reflection, was a sign for you to act or to change in some way? Keeping in mind that God's will for us always leads to our greatest joy, offer to God in prayer your willingness to receive such signs and to act on them.

3. What stood out for you in Jaime's story? What touched your heart the most?

4. In her message, Mary tells us, "You will not turn your head away from those who suffer, because my Son turns His head away from those who do so. Children, do not hesitate." Has a good work, an act of compassion, been on your mind and heart to do that you just haven't gotten around to? What has been stopping you, and

how can you use Jaime's story to help you take your next step forward?

5. The suffering in this world can feel overwhelming, and Papá Jaime has encountered some of the worst. Even when we are moving forward in a good work, everything can seem to come crashing down around and within us as the enemy tries to stop our efforts by placing obstacles in our way. Has this ever happened to you? What helps in such times to lift up your spirit and keep you going?

6. When the poor are out of sight, they are often out of mind. As Mother Teresa urged, we must go in search of them. Helping the poor is not an option for a Christian. It is a requirement. For when we neglect the poor, the Gospel says, we neglect God himself. In article 2446, the *Catechism of the Catholic Church* quotes these words from St. John Chrysostom: "Not to enable the poor to share in our goods is to steal from them and deprive them of life. The goods we possess are not ours, but theirs." "The demands of justice must be satisfied first of all; that which is already due in justice is not to be offered as a gift of charity." Jaime expressed a similar point when saying that storerooms with old, unused goods shouldn't even exist. What does St. John Chrysostom mean when he says that we should share our possessions as a necessary act of justice rather than one of charity? How might this perspective change your lifestyle?

FAITH EXERCISE

"God blesses those who come to the aid of the poor and rebukes those who turn away from them: 'Give to him who begs from you, do not refuse him who would borrow from you; you received without pay, give without pay.' (Mt 5:42; 10:8) It is by what they have done for the poor that Jesus Christ will recognize his chosen ones" (*Catechism of the Catholic Church*, 2443).

Take a moment to relax into prayer. With an openness of heart before Jesus, see him in your mind's eye, standing before you as the poor man that he was, and ask him directly: "Lord, how are you calling me to help the poor, the sick, the imprisoned, the cold, the hungry?" Wait in silence. If he speaks to your heart, do whatever he tells you.

FOUR

ANGELA

When God takes away the job she loves,
a stripper's growing devotion to Mary and
the rosary turns an angry, despondent woman
into a joyful warrior of prayer.

My sinful life started early. I was just doing the norm, everything my friends did. At fourteen, I met my first boyfriend,
who was eighteen. At fifteen, I started to have sex with him,
and at sixteen, I got pregnant. "I don't want to have a kid," I
thought to myself, and quickly had an abortion without realizing I was killing my child. Even though I had no idea what
I'd done, I cried a lot afterward and couldn't be around kids.
Every year after that, I remembered, "My child would be one,
or two, or three . . ."

Right when I got together with my boyfriend, problems
started with my father. He felt that my boyfriend was wrong
for me because of my age and his drinking. But I was in love
and didn't care. Whenever possible, I'd sneak out of the house,
and my father reacted by trying to run my boyfriend over with
the car.

On my seventeenth birthday, my father was going to give me permission to get a ride to school with my boyfriend, but I had disobeyed him by getting a ride the day before. That did it; my father threw me out of the house. He'd had enough of me and told me not to see my boyfriend anymore. My mother and brother went with me to a shelter. My father quickly found us and brought us back to our house in Massachusetts; but he still didn't want anything to do with me, and only spoke to me when he had to.

Even though I was the cause of everything wrong in my dad's eyes, he started using my mom as a scapegoat. My parents began to fight all the time. This kind of behavior wasn't completely new to me. Since I was little, my father had been verbally abusive toward my mother and sometimes slapped her. He was very controlling, and I was always scared. I grew up thinking that one of my parents would be dead and the other in jail from killing them. My mom, I figured, would probably be the one who ended up dead.

I Felt Abandoned

You could say I was raised Greek Orthodox, but my family never went to church, except for weddings and funerals. I knew nothing about God, Jesus, or the Blessed Mother. When my brother, who is two years younger than me, converted to Catholicism, I thought he was nuts, and we grew apart.

At age twenty-two, I found out that my long-time boyfriend had been cheating on me and doing drugs. Heartbroken and furious, I broke up with him. My parents broke up on the same day—Valentine's Day.

After that, I lost all trust in men and hated guys so much that I took up kick-boxing, spent a lot of time at the gym venting my rage, and considered taking anger management classes.

For the next ten years, if I found out a guy was cheating on me, I started punching him. And I didn't want too many friends because I'd lost trust in people. It seemed like no one had real, true love. The only person I trusted was my mom, whose name is Mary.

One day, my mom told me that my dad had cheated on her. When I heard this, my heart burned with extreme hatred for my dad. Then we found out much worse: he'd gotten a girl pregnant—someone younger than me—and had a son by her. At that point, my mom wouldn't let him back in the house. He and this girl stayed together and got married twelve years later. My dad was a cheater and a liar, and I wanted nothing to do with his new wife, his new son, or his stepdaughter. He replaced us, and I felt abandoned.

All through my childhood, I'd loved my dad and wanted to spend time with him, but whenever I tried to speak with him, my words set him off, and he'd yell at me or punish me. This made me so sad that we just stopped having conversations. And now he was gone.

I Started Doing Stripping Acts

After Dad left for good, I started clubbing, going out, dressing in sexy outfits, dating anyone, and sleeping around. My mother, brother, and I moved into a house I bought, and I ended up working at a nightclub in Massachusetts. At my new job, a fantasy of mine became real. I started doing stripping acts, taking everything off.

When I was dancing, I looked out at the men and didn't care about any of them. My eyes only focused on the dollar sign. All men, I figured, went to strip clubs—more than half the guys at my club were married. They'd tell their wives they were going shopping, then buy presents to give to the club girls, especially at Christmastime.

Listening to all the lies they told their wives made me sick. "Oh, my wife doesn't know I'm here. She doesn't understand me." Sometimes, after hearing enough, I told them they should spend more time with their wives. Other times, thinking of the money, I ignored what they said. I figured clubs like this shouldn't exist, but since they did, why shouldn't the money go in my pockets? What did it matter? I didn't trust anybody anyway. I just hated the whole world. But there was one thing I did love: my work.

My brother never had a clue what I was doing. He just thought I worked at a bar. But my mom ended up finding out and told me to quit stripping. Lashing back at her, I yelled, "I'm old enough for you not to tell me what to do!" I was making fifteen hundred dollars a week—only working Thursday, Friday, and Saturday—and planned to work at this job until retirement. In retaliation, I bought another house and moved out.

Without a sting of conscience, I continued with my job and fell in love again at age twenty-nine, with a new boyfriend who owned a nightclub. Constant arguments flew back and forth between us, especially because I didn't want him visiting the club where I worked and talking to other strippers; nor did I like going to his club because I fought with the girls there. One day, when my eye caught a married woman flirting with him, I walked over and punched her. But that wasn't enough, so I pulled her hair, kicked and slapped her, and called her names. The police charged me with assault and battery with a deadly weapon—my "shod foot"—and I had to go to court over it. They put me on probation for a year.

After that, I wouldn't go into his club anymore. He says he was faithful to me, but I doubt it. Nothing ever came from his promise to propose to me. While our love wasn't a question in my heart, trust always was.

The only happiness in my life was my work, because I got to dress up, look beautiful, and act sexy, while money and attention were thrown at me like candy. When I was dancing, I was a different person.

So that was my life before my conversion.

God Wants Me to Quit My Job

On Wednesday, June 7, as I was getting ready to go to work, an unexplainable force or feeling, like a wall, was put up inside me. It insisted that I not leave the house to go to work that day. Now, I just thought perhaps God was protecting me, that maybe I'd get into a fight at work or into a car accident and run off the side of the road—since I used to fall asleep while driving. At the very moment I felt the wall, I started saying out loud, "God won't let me go to work today. God won't let me go to work today."

The words made me cry. I was losing money and wanted to go do my job! Bored and restless, I consoled myself by figuring the next day would make up for it, as I sat with my mom at her home, watching TV.

The next day came, and the feeling that I shouldn't go to work got stronger. This time, I sensed God telling me to quit my job. Why God would want this, or what exactly was happening to me, I had no idea. Walking around the house alone, I just kept saying out loud, "God wants me to quit my job. God wants me to quit my job." At this point, my crying became hysterical. I'd taken a day off, but to quit was another thing. When

I called my mom to tell her what God wanted, she answered, "Good. I didn't like your job anyway."

Then my boyfriend called, and I told him the news. He didn't believe I would quit. Neither did my mom. No one believed me. And I just couldn't bring myself to call my work, so I avoided it, thinking, "Maybe tomorrow I'll feel different."

I didn't feel different, and I didn't go to work. The next day, Friday, June 9, I got an even stronger feeling that I had to quit, so I stayed at my mother's house, along with my brother, and cried some more. Now I was missing big money.

Then on Saturday, I felt that God wanted me to stop taking birth control pills. I don't know how I knew to stop, because I hadn't read or heard anything about it being wrong or that it could abort a baby. Without understanding the reasons why, I told my boyfriend I was going to stop taking the pill. At this time in my life, I started getting a sense of God's desires; and whatever I sensed, I said, and then did.

That night, after two days of stalling, I finally got the courage to call my boss and quit. Now I had no job and no idea why God had wanted this. I felt miserable and confused.

I Said I Was a Sinner

Father's Day was coming up the next week, Sunday, June 18, and I had already decided I wasn't going to visit my father. Instead, my plans were to emotionally disown him. At the same time, something inside of me told me I had to go to church on that Sunday. While I was wondering what church to go to, I overheard my mother talking to my aunt, who went to an Assemblies of God church, so I told my aunt I wanted to go with her.

We sat together in the back of the church, and when the reverend started preaching, I felt like he was talking directly to me: "If you feel like you're called to be here today, God has a reason for it. . . . If you need to be cleansed, come up to the altar."

"I need to go up there," I whispered to my aunt. Then I stood up and walked forward, crying the whole way. Kneeling down in front of the altar, I said I was a sinner. The words just came out of my mouth, without my knowing what they meant.

When I left the church, I started to read a tiny pocket New Testament that my brother had given me, and as I did, I sensed God asking me to forgive my father. Drained from crying so much at church, I had no energy to visit him that day, so I called him up, wished him a happy Father's Day, and told him I wanted to see him.

The very next day, my father came over to my house. Striking up a conversation with him, I mentioned how I'd gone to church and handed him a picture of Mary. Then I looked intently at him and said, "I forgive you." But he wasn't willing to admit any wrongdoing. Old feelings of anger and upset rose up inside of me, and I realized I should've just told him that I loved him and let the past go. So, pushing my hurt feelings aside, I continued to have a nice Father's Day. Before he left, I gave him a hug, said I'd come visit him, and suggested we go to church together.

The following Sunday, my father and I went to his Greek Orthodox church, along with his two kids—a boy and a girl, ages eleven and eight. Although I still had a hard time talking to his wife, I started talking to the kids—the first time I ever acknowledged them. That day began a tradition of regular visits to my dad's home. And that day, in my heart, I truly forgave my father and welcomed him back into my life.

God Wants Me to Forgive You

On June 21, the Wednesday after Trinity Sunday, I felt a strong pull to call the married girl at my boyfriend's club, the one I'd beaten up in the fight that sent me to court. Every single day since I'd caught her flirting with him a year earlier, she was on my mind. As much as I'd hated my dad, I still hated this girl. Whenever her name came up, it made me sick, and I was always mad at my boyfriend for never firing her. It was very hard for me to reach out to her, but that day, when I called my boyfriend's bar, she just happened to pick up the phone. I didn't even know what day she worked, so when she answered, I felt that the conversation was meant to happen.

She was probably scared when I said who I was. "I'm calling you," I said, "because I felt like God wanted me to forgive you and to tell you I'm sorry for treating you so badly. Please accept my apology."

Then she started crying and said, "Oh, no, it was my fault. I was the one who was wrong, and I deserved it."

My boyfriend called me back, shortly after I'd hung up with her, and said, "She's crying, and she told me she just talked to you. What did you say to her? Are you starting in on her again?"

"No. I just called up to say I was sorry."

"What? What did you go and do that for? You didn't have to do that."

Then I just knew and thought to myself, "Ah, so there really was something going on!" After that day, she went back to church. She also ended up quitting her job at the club.

This was still just two weeks after my conversion.

"I'm Going Out Dancing Tonight"

Without my job, I didn't know what to do with myself. Another day passed, and I got unbearably restless. Remembering that my mother and I had tried country western dancing and liked it, I said spontaneously one evening, "I'm going out dancing tonight."

My brother overheard me. "I'll take you out dancing," he said, and invited me to go out with him and a friend of his, who was thinking about becoming a nun. So she came by and picked us up to go dancing. At least I thought it was dancing. What it turned out to be was a charismatic prayer group. When I got there, they were praying the rosary. Then they had a Mass. Then, after the Mass, they got up to dance and sing in tongues. That's the dancing my brother had in mind.

During the prayer service, which lasted all evening and into the night, I got hungry and had something to eat. I noticed that the girl who wanted to be a nun wouldn't eat when we offered her food. I asked my brother why not, and he said she was fasting on Wednesdays and Fridays. "What does she fast for?" I asked.

"The Blessed Mother wants people to fast," he answered.

"Well, I want to fast, too, then," I said, and began fasting on bread and water on Wednesdays and Fridays. The girl also gave me a book on the rosary, telling me that the Blessed Mother wants us to pray the rosary every day. So the very next day, when I was walking my dogs, I practiced, trying hard to memorize the prayers. The rosary didn't mean anything to me at the time, though. My heart didn't match my words because I didn't yet know how to pray.

"I Love You, Mother Mary"

On July 2, I went to the beach with my boyfriend, and we were going to make love after we got home, but I stopped him and said, "I can't do this anymore." The thought of having sex didn't feel right, and I just knew we weren't supposed to. I'd been saying the rosary every day now for a couple of weeks. My boyfriend hung in there with me, but let me know he thought I was going too far—quitting my job; dressing more conservatively; fasting; saying the rosary; wearing Catholic medals, my latest fashion addition; and now, no sex.

By this point, just three and a half weeks after my conversion, a love for Mary began to grow in my heart, and I started saying out loud, "I love you, Mother Mary." I bought four roses for her, two pink and two white, and put them in my room. And while saying the rosary daily still wasn't easy, it was something I could do for her. So I continued, and, over time, my heart caught up with the prayers. It was easy for me to love Mother Mary, maybe because it was so easy for me to love my own mother, Mary, who always stood by me. I also started saying "I love you" to Jesus, but, perhaps because he was a man, my heart struggled to feel the words.

Then I sensed that God wanted me to record everything, so I noted what was happening to me on a calendar and began writing in a daily journal. Soon after that, I received the desire to read the Bible and pulled out my little pocket New Testament every day to read its tiny writing. My faith was growing.

At the charismatic service, I'd heard that angels liked to pray for us, so I learned the Guardian Angel Prayer and started saying it before going to bed every night. Then, all of a sudden, I got the gift of joy. As I lay in bed at night, I would start laughing and couldn't stop. It was a supernatural feeling, and I wasn't laughing at anything in particular. Something inside was filling me up with joy and causing me to giggle. This gift of extreme joy stayed with me for two whole years, during which I was always smiling and happy and talking about Mary.

Two months after my conversion, I decided that I wanted to become Catholic, so I joined the Rite of Christian Initiation for Adults (RCIA) program. Only then did I learn about the sins of the flesh and realize how lost my soul had been. Many times I thought, "Wow, that's a sin?" as the truth was revealed to me. I started thanking God every day, every single day, for saving me and changing my heart. Before RCIA, I didn't know anything about the Bible, or about heaven, hell, and purgatory. I didn't realize that in the life I'd been leading—with the stripping, the sex before marriage, the anger—I'd had one foot in hell. When I'd gotten the abortion, I didn't know any better, and finding out the truth was a painful process. A soul was meant to be born, and I didn't give it that chance. I was going to healing services, and that helped me deal with it. I focused a lot on God's forgiveness.

I'm Going to Go to Medjugorje

When the end of August came, I got the feeling I should sell my house. Now, I loved my house. It was fixed up just the way I liked it—perfect for me. But I sensed God telling me, "It's time to sell your house," so, with a huge sigh, I started packing up my things.

"Why are you packing your house now?" my mom asked. "It takes time to sell a house."

"I've got to clean it out now," I said. "If God wants me to sell the house, I know it will sell fast." So I started bringing boxes over to my mother's house, and in September, put the house up for sale. This was extremely painful for me, but I obeyed God.

My spontaneous knowledge of things continued. For about a month, I'd been thinking to myself, "I'm going to go to Medjugorje," and sometimes said it out loud. One day, while looking at a flyer about a Marian charismatic renewal conference coming up in October, I said, "I'm going to be in Medjugorje on the feast of the Holy Rosary." This just came out of my mouth, and I didn't even know when that feast day was.

My mom was now finding me as strange as my boyfriend did. When I told her my plans she said, "Yeah, yeah, yeah. What day do you think you're gonna leave?"

"I should leave October 5," I said. This date flew out of my mouth, too. Later, I happened to look at a calendar and saw that the feast of the Holy Rosary was on October 7, the day I said I would be there. Meanwhile, I hadn't made any arrangements to go, and it was already September. Looking through the conference flyer again, I saw a phone number, called it, and asked if they knew about Medjugorje.

"We take people there," they said, "and we have a trip leaving on October 5."

"I'm supposed to be on that trip," I said. "Go ahead and book me."

My mother looked shocked. The trip was on the same date that I said I was going to leave. Then she grumbled, "I can't believe you just booked a trip without a passport."

"I'm telling you, Mom," I said, "Mother Mary wants me to go to Medjugorje, so God will get me my passport." I got my passport two days before I left. I was never worried. I had such faith. I don't know where it came from.

I told my mother, "My house is going to sell before I go to Medjugorje."

"Houses don't sell that fast."

"Yes, it will. If God wants it to sell, it's gonna sell. God wants me to sell my furniture, too," I said—and I loved my furniture. "I'll just include it in the price of the house."

"People who buy houses don't want furniture."

"I'm telling you, whoever buys this house will want the furniture, too, and I will be living with you by November 1."

My mom didn't know what to say at this point, except for, "Yeah, yeah, yeah." Then she asked me, "What if they want to talk you down in price while you're gone?"

"They're going to buy my house and pay full price," I answered.

My house sold in one week. The people who bought it paid full price, wanted the furniture, and asked to live there by October 31.

I Felt Inspired

I traveled to Medjugorje just after the house sold. I loved it there and didn't want to come home. Mary's sweet presence was everywhere, and I felt like I belonged. Wherever I went, people were praying the rosary, and the whole town seemed to go to Mass. I remember how packed the church was, how patient and caring the priests were, and how lovingly people helped each other up Cross Mountain and Apparition Hill. Most of all, I remember how peaceful it was.

In Medjugorje, I felt that I should confess all the sins from my life. In the confessional, I told the priest that I wasn't a Catholic, but I was in the RCIA program, and with patience and kindness, he listened to my many sins and gave me comfort. Later on that day, he even invited me to join up with his tour group to give a testimony, because he knew some of the girls in his group also had problems with their fathers. So I shared my story, and he told me that it helped them to forgive.

Since it rained every day I was there, our pilgrimage group didn't hike up Cross Mountain or Apparition Hill together. Deciding to go myself, I climbed up each of them in the rain. I even slept on Cross Mountain one night, and had this crazy idea that Jesus might visit me. Someone walked up the hill in the middle of the night, and I thought it might be him, so I screamed and startled the poor person.

Just three months after my conversion, instead of stripping in a nightclub, I was across the world, sleeping on top of a mountain, in the rain, in a country where the Blessed Mother was appearing, wondering if Jesus might show up.

When I came back from Medjugorje, I felt inspired to teach everyone the rosary and to pray it more. I remembered how God had wanted me in Medjugorje on the feast of the Holy Rosary, and now I understood why—how important this was. Mother Mary is asking all of us to say at least one rosary each day, especially with our families. In one of her messages, she says, "Even the rosary alone can work miracles in the world and in your lives" (January 25, 1991). She repeats again and again, "Pray, pray, pray," and I wanted to pray, pray, pray. If she has to keep telling us this, obviously we're not listening.

Something Supernatural Was Happening

When January came around, I went on a weekend Cursillo retreat. It was a wonderful short course in Christianity, and an encounter with Jesus, a chance to know him better. On that weekend, I finally fell in love with him.

Before then, I knew I was supposed to love Jesus before all else, but I didn't know how. Even though I often looked at the picture of the Sacred Heart of Jesus and told Jesus I loved him, I didn't feel anything like love. During the Cursillo weekend, after the retreat's healing service, Jesus caught my attention by physically tapping me on the shoulder. In my heart, I heard him say, "You know how you think about your boyfriend all the time? You know the love that you have for him, the way you always want to please him, make him happy, do nice things for him? I want you to love me that way." Then it hit me. Jesus died on a cross for me. At that moment, he opened my eyes to see how much he loves me, how much he loves us all. And the peace that he always said he'd give . . . I felt that peace. Jesus healed my hardened heart, and I responded with great love. After that, whenever I thought about Jesus, I felt happy.

When you love somebody, you want to be around that person all the time, so I started going to Mass every day. I wanted to hear, through the Scripture readings, what Jesus had to say. Everything that was being proclaimed—"Love one another," "Forgive your enemies"—I tried to go out and live. God's Word brought me such joy. After Jesus entered my heart, he was always on my mind and in my words. I talked about him all the time, saying to people, "Jesus loves you. Jesus loves you."

Just after the Cursillo weekend, I decided to read a Christian book I'd bought at the retreat. When I opened the book, a surge of good energy caught me by surprise and began flowing from the pages and through my hands. Drawn to the book and hungry to learn from Jesus and be with him, I stayed up reading until three in the morning. Through the prayers in the book, I felt Jesus saying to me that he loved me and wanted me to work for him. I said yes and told him, "I will do anything you ask of me. I surrender my will to you."

Then I closed the book and fell asleep. About twenty minutes later, electricity suddenly began to run through my entire body. Terrified, I thought I was being electrocuted; but at the same time, I sensed something supernatural might be happening. I kept my eyes closed, worried it would stop if I opened them. Loud ringing pounded in my ears, and a strong jolt of electricity rattled in my head. And then, with the eyes of my soul, I saw the outline of a figure appear at the foot of my bed. I couldn't make out any details, but I knew who it was—a person very familiar to me. "Mother Mary!" I called out. "It's really you! I see you. I love you. You came to visit me. I'm so happy."

Then the electricity raced through me more powerfully, and in my head, I could feel and hear a loud, vibrating sound, exactly like a tape rewinding. I saw images of people in my mind, laughing and having a good time, like they were at a party, but I didn't recognize anybody. As the "tape" rewound, I didn't see anything of my life, although I half expected to.

Then Mother Mary left, and in her place, standing at the foot of my bed, was Jesus. My soul recognized him, although the details of his facial features were hidden. He extended his hand before me—a very large hand that he placed right in front of my face and over my head. An extreme heat came from his hand, and my face felt like it was on fire. This lasted seconds, but it was so painful! I thought that if I looked in the mirror, my face would appear black and charred, so I didn't dare open my eyes, but allowed my face to continue burning, with the thought that I was being purified in order to grow more holy, to be more like Jesus.

Then behind Jesus, a large wooden cross appeared and then vanished, three times in a row. After that, I didn't see or feel anything. I just lay in my bed with my eyes closed, hoping another vision would appear.

I wanted it all to happen again. I didn't care what pain I went through. After waiting a long time, I reluctantly opened my eyes. Getting up, I called my boyfriend to leave the details on his machine and told him not to erase it, so I could remember my experience the next day.

I knew what happened wasn't a dream but something from heaven. Jesus and Mary had just visited me, and it was all I could think of. Over and over, I kept saying, "I love you, Jesus. I love you, Mary. Whatever you want me to do, I'll do. Let me do more for you." Excited and overjoyed, I couldn't wait to tell my mom and my brother about my experience. I just wanted to tell everybody. At Mass at St. Mary's Church the next day, I couldn't hold in the news, so I ran to the priest, excited and out of breath, and told him about the vision. Then I blurted out, "I want to receive the Eucharist now—I'd like to be Catholic now." I was already going through the RCIA program, but I didn't want to wait until Easter.

He thought I was nuts, I'm sure, and politely said, "Let's see if there's any fruit from this." But I couldn't wait, so I wrote to the cardinal, "I have a strong desire to receive Jesus. I sense that Jesus wants me to receive him now. I feel Jesus talking to me when I am at Mass in the Roman Catholic Church, and I want to complete this feeling by receiving him. Since I feel at home in the Roman Catholic Church, and I do believe in the pope, I would like to become a Roman Catholic as soon as possible."

On January 23, the archdiocese wrote a letter to St. Mary's. I still have it. It says, "I am pleased to inform you that permission is granted for you to be received into full communion with the Catholic Church as a member of the Latin Church in accord with Canon 32.2 of the Code of Cannons of the Eastern Churches."

On February 12, I became Catholic. On that day at St. Mary's Church, I stood up at Mass and said a profession of faith. In their bulletin they congratulated me on becoming a full member of their church. I was so happy. I felt like this was where I belonged.

I Feel Extreme Joy

How I feel now doesn't compare to anything I've ever felt before. I feel free as a butterfly. I used to have so much anger within me that I clenched my fists during the day, but now peace is in my heart. I never feel stress anymore. It's gone. I don't feel hatred for anybody, just love. Before, I didn't trust anyone, but now I look for Jesus in people and have a lot of Christian friends I can trust. Before, I didn't know God, and now I'm in love with him. Before, I never went to church, and now I look forward to going to Mass every day.

Before my conversion, I refused to even talk to my father. I am so thankful for God's graces that helped me to forgive him and create a good relationship with him. My dad died about two and a half years after I became Catholic, and now my prayers will help get him out of purgatory and into heaven. Before I wouldn't have known how to help him, or that I could even help him at all.

In the past, I wouldn't have anything to do with my dad's second family, and today our relationship is close. My mother gets along with my dad's wife now, and everything is peaceful between our families. We even spend Christmas together.

My mom, who was a non-practicing Catholic, has been going to Mass with me every Sunday. My boyfriend, who just recently started going to daily Mass, tells me, "I want to get married, and you're bringing me closer to God." But we'll see. All I want to do is be with Jesus. I want to take care of the sick, the elderly, and the dying, which is my job now as a home health aide. There are so many people in need.

To be closer to Jesus, you have to carry a heavy cross, but I haven't received one yet. I don't think I have any crosses. I'm too happy. But I'll take whatever he gives me. The only thing that bothers and saddens me is when I look at the world and see that people don't pray. They don't love God. We do things like go to war and kill each other over power, money, and religion. I wish people would just stop what they're doing. I want so much for others to know God. If it's going to mean my suffering for others, so be it. I'll be single, married, a nun. I'll do whatever God wants.

Nowadays, my focus is God. He's on my mind, in my heart, and on my lips, which constantly praise him. I go to daily Mass, say three rosaries a day, do Bible reading, spend time in Eucharistic adoration, pray the Divine Mercy Chaplet at three o'clock, and fast on bread and water on Wednesdays and Fridays. This is what I feel God wants for me. Plus I tell him all day that I love him. When I'm doing all these things, I feel extreme joy.

We don't really know what makes us happy. We look for eternal joy, but nothing ever lasts. Jesus stays. His peace and fulfillment stays. It doesn't go away. It's what we've always desired. We're part of him, and we're not truly happy until we live in him, talk with him—love him.

I have complete faith now in God. It's amazing to really feel faith and live it. Since my conversion, I walk out of the house and say, "Ahhh, I have nothing to worry about. God is with me."

Dear children! With the time of Lent, you are approaching a time of grace. Your heart is like ploughed soil, and it is ready to receive the fruit which will grow into what is good. You, little children, are free to choose good or evil. Therefore, I call you to pray and fast. Plant joy and the fruit of joy will grow in your hearts for your good, and others will see it and receive it through your life. Renounce sin and choose eternal life. I am with you and intercede for you before my Son. Thank you for having responded to my call.

—Mary's message of January 25, 2008, from www.medjugorje.ws

FOR PRAYERFUL REFLECTION

By the grace of God, Angela escaped slavery to sin by dying to one desire after another. Moving reluctantly at first, then with a beautiful, childlike fervor, she became a slave to God, obedient from the heart to the teachings of Christ. These words from St. Paul could just as easily been written to her.

> Therefore, sin must not reign over your mortal bodies so that you obey their desires. And do not present the parts of your bodies to sin as weapons for wickedness, but present yourselves to God as raised from the dead to life and the parts of your bodies to God as weapons for righteousness. For sin is not to have any power over you, since you are not under the law but under grace.
>
> What then? Shall we sin because we are not under the law but under grace? Of course not! Do you not know that if you present yourselves to someone as obedient slaves, you are slaves of the one you obey, either of sin, which leads to death, or of obedience, which leads to righteousness? But

> thanks be to God that, although you were once
> slaves of sin, you have become obedient from the
> heart to the pattern of teaching to which you were
> entrusted. Freed from sin, you have become slaves
> of righteousness.
>   For the wages of sin is death, but the gift of
> God is eternal life in Christ Jesus our Lord.
>
> —Romans 6:12–18, 23

1. Angela's life literally enfleshes this passage from St. Paul. Although sin once reigned over her mortal body, she became obedient to the pattern of teaching to which she was entrusted. God communicated his will again and again directly to Angela's soul, and without the least bit of understanding on her part, she obeyed. Can you recall an occasion when God communicated his will to you? Was it easy to obey? Did you struggle with fear or resistance? What was the outcome of doing—or not doing—what he asked?

2. What is God showing you personally through Angela's story and Mary's message?

3. Angela had hated, with a vengeance, her father and the woman at her boyfriend's club. Even so, she extended her forgiveness toward them, despite the fact that her father never admitted any guilt and the woman alluded to wrongdoing only after she was forgiven. Do you find it easy or hard to forgive others, and why? How do you believe others see you: as someone who holds grudges? harbors no ill will? is resentful? easily forgives?

4. Angela's story begins, "My sinful life started early. I was just doing the norm, everything my friends did." Angela's past sins included premarital sex, birth control, abortion, and stripping. In many ways, American culture presents these sins as the norm. Do any other sins come to mind that have become "normal" today? How do you respond when people you care about engage in activities that are clearly not God's way? What difficulties or fears arise when you try to broach the uncomfortable subject of sin in the lives of others?

What has worked best for you in helping others toward a more Godly lifestyle?

5. How close do you feel to the Father and the Son? How close do you feel to Mary? How do your relationships with each of them reflect—both positively and negatively—your past relationships with your parents or guardians? Make a list of qualities that you've witnessed and experienced in your parents or guardians. Notice if you've projected any of those same traits onto the Father, or the Son, or onto Mary. Do you hold any unforgiveness toward them that could be a reflection of unforgiveness toward those who raised you? If any projections or resentments are discovered, ask Mary to gently untangle your view and free you to know and love her and God more completely.

6. In the past, Angela's stripping job was the only thing that made her happy. Now her happiness comes from God. What brings you joy?

FAITH EXERCISE

There's so much to learn about the Catholic faith, and most of us know only snippets of information that we assume to be correct. Once a new fact is learned or a new thought ingested, sometimes what the Church teaches can seem more reasonable or doable than we may have once believed. Angela obeyed God's commands without knowing why. That isn't so easy for most people. This coming week, read the writings of a person who has researched and is explaining or defending a particular Church teaching. Choose one that you find difficult to understand, or from which you may dissent. Ask the Holy Spirit to be with you and guide you as you read.

FIVE

MICHAEL

Through eyes turned hollow from an addiction to cocaine, a former altar boy from a good family follows a brilliant light in Medjugorje to his freedom.

Although my parents weren't wealthy, I grew up in an affluent San Francisco neighborhood of two- and three-story houses, each one architecturally unique and with a beautifully sculpted yard. In this enclave of material abundance, I hung out with the cool kids who experimented with drugs and had the money to get them. Although unaware of it at the time, I was in a heated competition over the material world—what bike you rode, what clothes you wore. None of my friends had to work for their money, so I—devoid of any concept of earning or responsibility and averse to the idea of work or discipline—learned, at a very young age, the fine art of parental manipulation. If I wanted something, I would get it. If I couldn't manipulate, I would steal. If I got caught, I would lie. For instance, when I was eleven, it never occurred to me that it was wrong to talk my parents into buying me a $500 bicycle. I amazed even myself at what I could get them to do.

As a boy who was naturally hooked on adrenaline, I used to throw rocks at cop cars to make them chase me and jump out of high windows and trees just for the rush of excitement. I lived in the moment of satisfying each immediate desire as my family, friends, neighbors, parents, and acquaintances searched for their missing money and possessions. Even though I got caught all the time, I never learned from it. My parents punished me, but their consequences never stuck. I enjoyed keeping them on their toes, ducking their chastisements with humor and sweetness, as they dealt with the consequences of my latest stunt.

Other than the trouble I caused, I had a very good family life. Yet even with my caring mother, father, and a squeaky-clean model sister, I suffered emotionally. My blows came from peers and began in my first grammar school, where I barely survived a class of an exceptionally rotten bunch of kids—the worst, teachers said, that ever passed through that school.

One instance that happened in the schoolyard probably changed the way I went through life. While other kids watched, a horrible, nasty little boy in my class slammed my head up against the wall; and instead of using my adrenaline to retaliate, I walked away crying. Before then, I had never been rough-housed. Growing up without a brother, I didn't expect it, didn't understand it, didn't even know it existed, and certainly didn't want any part of it. As a result, the other kids saw my weakness and zeroed in on their new target.

My humiliation began to fester as an underlying fear of everything. From the time I opened my eyes in the morning to the time I drifted into sleep at night, my thoughts tortured me with a sickening feeling of intense anxiety: "I haven't done my homework. . . . The bully will get me. . . . I can't face the day. . . ."

I Had Become What I Hated Most

My temper started to flare both in school and after school, and I acted out my anger through vandalism and fights. After being transferred to another grammar school at age ten, I established my domination to avoid future humiliation. I became an aggressor, ready to punch a kid in the face just because he was weak. I chased one student around the playground with the calculated intention of pummeling him with my fists. Failing to grasp him, I felt satisfied by his look of abject fear. By age eleven, I had become what I hated most.

That year I also began to drink alcohol, which temporarily allowed me to be my preferred persona—cool and comfortable. All my fears dissolved after a few bottles of beer. A peer had already introduced me to *Playboy* when I was eight, and another had just started listening to heavy metal bands, which used satanic logos like Pentagrams and upside down crosses.

By the time I was fourteen, my T-shirts and bedroom walls were covered with Black Sabbath, Ozzy Osbourne, and Iron Maiden. I wore a walkman most of the time and plugged myself into MTV, so I knew every word to every heavy metal song. The power, rhythm, and popularity of the music drew me in. I read a lot of rock and roll magazines and learned of how, in concert, KISS, Iron Maiden, and Ozzy Osbourne bit the heads off of doves and bats and stomped on puppies. They oozed with pure evil. "I don't believe in this," I said to myself, "but what am I going to do about it? Everyone else is listening to this stuff."

Something mysterious and exciting came with crossing moral boundaries. I felt the allure of darkness and of the lifestyle that went along with the music. After first trying alcohol at eleven, I smoked cigarettes at twelve, then marijuana at thirteen. Dancing with the devil, I thought that by recognizing evil, I was somehow above it.

Yet inside, I brewed with turmoil because I knew what I was doing was wrong. I had always been adamantly against drugs, against anything of the devil, but once I compromised one conviction in a seemingly insignificant way, it was easy to compromise another, and another. Over time, I decided to get high on almost a daily basis to silence my conscience. I was building a staircase downward.

"I'll Break Your Neck If You Do Drugs"

My parents sent me to psychologists and neurological doctors, beginning at age ten, to see why I wouldn't try in school. I knew why . . . I simply didn't want to. I just wanted to be free, free from all responsibility. I had no goals and therefore needed no preparation. I didn't care that I was asked to leave eight different San Francisco schools by age seventeen. My parents wanted an answer to something for which there was perhaps no medical or easy psychological explanation.

All my tests came out perfectly. I had a natural aptitude for absorbing information, scoring high on IQ tests and normal on all other psychological tests. So, it was left a mystery to everyone why I just sat and daydreamed in school, frittering away my time drawing cartoons and logos.

No one knew about the drugs. My secrets were dark, and I felt ashamed. I trusted no one with them. As my parents threw big money on psychologists and doctors who gave me diagnoses of clinical depression and, later, anti-social personality disorder, I remained closed.

My mom, a docile, sweet-tongued woman, told me emphatically, "I'll break your neck if you do drugs." That's just how strongly she felt. My dad didn't speak the rules, but he didn't have to. We just knew them.

My parents had grown up in a different era, having had me later in life. When my mom was thirty-five years old, she asked my dad, "What does "f---" mean?"

"What?" he responded. "You've gotta be kidding me!"

That was the world they lived in. They knew people swore and did drugs, but never themselves nor their kids. My parents loved me without knowing me. They couldn't protect me from myself or the evil around me because they couldn't see who I really was. My inner life lay hidden in their denial.

Meanwhile, I served as an altar boy at Mass on Sunday, enjoyed church, and sang in the San Francisco Boys' Chorus with a perfect soprano voice. A couple nights a week, I knelt with my sister and my parents next to their bed, praying the rosary. All the while, unbeknownst to me, my conscience was suffocating. While I doubted many things, I never doubted anything I was taught about the doctrine of the Catholic faith. But I didn't feel the great defiance within me, as I lived one life at home and another with my friends. It didn't seem possible to carry on my beliefs and upbringing outside of the home and Church, so I didn't bother. Never contemplating where I was headed, I simply did and went where people and places took me.

Yet, for all the things I have done and experienced, I retained a strange innocence. Maliciousness never crept into my personality. My mother had half the world praying for me, which may have kept me from partaking in the depths of evil surrounding me. Some of my friends didn't escape from it. One of them is a pornography actor now. Another did seven years in prison for murder. Another is badly addicted to speed and served time in prison. Another killed old people for money. Whenever things were getting worse, I somehow knew to pull out. Despite our heavy substance use, only three of us got pulled into addiction. But I happened to be one of them.

Right From the Start, I Was Addicted

When I was sixteen, two of my friends became heavily involved in cocaine. Afraid, I resisted. I felt marijuana was one thing to try, but cocaine graduated into hardcore drug use. For almost two years, I urged my two friends to stop taking it. But one day, at age eighteen, while drunk at a house party, I walked into the garage where my two friends were chopping a pile of coke on a mirror, and without thinking, I said, "Let me get one of those." I did a line and almost immediately sobered up. I felt great.

I was a very quiet, introspective person by nature, lacking self-confidence, but suddenly I had social skills in abundance. That white powder was the magic line that made me feel the way I had always wanted to. "Why didn't I ever try this before?" I wondered to myself.

When the effects of the drug wore off a half hour later, I sat down next to my two friends at the house bar and asked them for another line. They said they didn't have any more. What happened next stands out strongly in my memory. I said to them, "I'm going to get some next weekend." One turned to look at the other. They didn't say anything, but I could see on their faces a strange look of guilty horror. "Did they know something I didn't?"

Right from the start, I was addicted. I didn't even wait a week to get high. As soon as I discovered their cocaine connection, I got more. My friends did the drug at parties; I did it any time during the day.

By now, I had dropped out of high school due to my grades, and I wasn't going back. Instead, I got in my car and drove around looking for people with whom I could socialize and get high. I stole money to support my habit—primarily from my parents. All the while I had no idea I was addicted. I just knew that cocaine made me feel whole, and I wanted to feel that way all the time.

People in recovery say, "I thought I could stop at any time." But I never intended to stop. I fancied myself part of an elite group that possessed a special, higher knowledge than most people. Everyone I knew drank, but not everybody used cocaine. People didn't know what they were missing. Many who have tried cocaine say that they either don't like it, or it doesn't do anything for them. I didn't know I was having a unique physiological, psychological, and spiritual reaction to it.

Cocaine lifted me out of my melancholy. Days possessed promise, and nights never ended. Many times I watched the sunrise, having sat up through the night talking with friends about such brilliant items as our grand plan to build a cabin in the woods. We delegated tasks: wood-carriers, architects, and construction experts. "You bring the nails. I'll bring the hammer." We were going to have a dock extending over a lake. It all made sense. Why wouldn't we build a cabin in the woods? We had the energy for it, and everyone felt euphoric and jazzed about the idea. No one had a single thought of, "This is ridiculous."

I had several cocaine sources, all in good neighborhoods where I felt safe. Each dealer welcomed me into his normal, middle- to upper-class home; he pulled out a scale; he weighed some white powder in the middle of a short, friendly conversation; he sold me the drug; and sometimes he even threw in a complimentary drink or a joint. In my moments of generosity, I then shared some of my purchase with the dealer.

The first two years that I used cocaine I had several fleeting jobs, from kitchen construction to parking cars in a lot. I never stayed for long. Once I got my first paycheck, I left and spent it to get high. During that time, the only negative effect of cocaine I could sense was the price; although one early afternoon as I sat in my car chopping coke on a mirror, I distinctly remember thinking, "This is going to be a problem." But the thought disappeared and was quickly replaced with euphoria.

My Parents Wanted to Believe My Lies

My family, which had always been close, soon became divided. My sister and I stopped talking to each other. We started yelling instead. Even my parents began to fight, and I had never before seen them bicker. "Are you blind?!" my sister would say to them. "Look at him! He's on drugs! Can't you see? He's even sweating!" My weight loss, sunken eyes, bloody noses, and protruding cheekbones vanished in my parents' trusting eyes. I was still the son who could do no wrong. I could sit in front of them, sweating profusely and with dilated pupils, and convince them I'd had too much coffee. I knew how to play them like a fine fiddle, and they remained codependent with me up until the end.

As much as they stayed in denial, they had to have known by my behavior that something was wrong. Once my mother said, "Please tell me you're on drugs, because if you're not, you've lost your mind." Everyone was waiting for the chaos to end, but it never did. After putting my family through yet another dramatic episode, I would promise better behavior, my parents would be full of hope, everything would smooth over for a few days, and then their world would explode again. They would miss another two hundred dollars, or find a straw, a rolled-up dollar bill, or a little plastic drug bag, and I would tell them:

"No, no. I'm not on drugs."

"But so-and-so told me they saw you using drugs."

"Oh, you know why? Because he's on drugs, and he's lying to deflect from getting caught."

Being so naïve about the drug culture, my parents wanted to believe my lies, and I was never going to tell them the truth. The truth was unthinkable for them. After months of seeing their checking account dwindle, their credit card bills skyrocket, and hearing stories that didn't add up, my parents looked me in the eye one day and questioned where the money had gone. Out of the blue, I came up with the idea that I had a certain problem: I was the world's worst gambler, and I never won any money. It seemed like a great alternative to being a drug addict.

"Oh, no wonder."

They believed me for about a week, until my dad said, "Wait a minute. I've never seen you with the sports page in your hand." I changed the subject.

One week later, they found the cocaine. At age twenty, passed out on my bed after a three-day binge, I peered through blurry eyes to see my father standing over me with the evidence. After searching my room high and low while I was asleep, my parents eventually unrolled the socks in my drawer and found a bag of coke. Filled with horror, they took the bag to a family friend, a police officer, who confirmed their fear. When I awoke, I was met with the words, "Get up, and get dressed. You're going to rehab." That isn't something you want to hear after emerging from a coma.

My father had also called a priest friend of his who knew about recovery centers in the area, and my parents insisted I speak with him that same morning. We sat in strained silence as my parents drove me to Lake Merced to meet him. Fear of the unknown caused a million dreadful thoughts to pass through my mind. All I knew of rehab was what I'd seen on TV: horrible, antiseptic settings with insane people walking around in hospital gowns. When we met the priest, I told him I was in no condition to stroll around Lake Merced talking, as he had suggested, and I was in no mood or state to be out in public, so we chatted for several minutes alone in the car.

The only thing I recall from our conversation was his earnest comment: "Just remember that you're sick and not evil." I didn't fully understand what he meant, because I had no idea how sick I was, but I held on to those words because I knew deep down that I wasn't evil. The things I did in order to get drugs were a result of my addiction, not my deeper self.

I found the priest very understanding and sound. I think he brought peace into the situation, into me, and into my parents. Many people's perception of drug addicts is that they've betrayed you, that they've somehow chosen drugs over family—"If you loved us, you would just stop. How could you do this to us?" The priest explained to my parents that I was suffering from the disease of addiction—that nobody wants to be an alcoholic or a drug addict.

For me, that day of discovery marked a dark moment. Overwhelming feelings of helplessness mixed with shame, remorse, and panic flooded my mind and body; but I didn't even think to defend myself because I knew the jig was up—my game was over. At the same time, underneath my dread was a sense of relief. I was thirty pounds underweight; I had been doing cocaine for weeks straight without a rest; and I was malnourished, dehydrated, destroyed. For four years I had been keeping my secrets, entangling myself in a huge web of deceit, and I didn't have to do that anymore. The façade had cracked.

I Didn't Want a Total Overhaul

Surprisingly, rehab wasn't at all what I had expected. Located in a beautiful setting in the mountains of Marin, with friendly staff and clients, the center helped me to feel less like a leper. I went swimming in the pool for fun, got a girlfriend and a tan, and kicked back with no worldly cares or daily responsibilities. Life was good, and everybody seemed happy with me again. My nice little three-month vacation also gave me a chance to recover my health and to learn about AA. But the lessons didn't take. I wasn't in enough pain—yet.

I was told that if I didn't get sober, I would have to experience a lot of suffering: jail, rehab, detox centers, halfway houses, institutions, hospitals. They called these things the "yets." Still holding onto alcohol and my own ideas of how to live, I didn't want to immerse myself in AA. I didn't want a total overhaul, a restructuring of my life, my friends, my social outlets, my habits. I was twenty-one. I was invincible.

The day I left the rehabilitation center, I cracked open a beer with old friends. I did attend some AA meetings with my new friends from rehab, where I got to know one guy particularly well. But neither of us had achieved a point of surrender, so one night we agreed we would get some coke together. In the blink of an eye, I went from snorting powder cocaine to smoking it—"freebasing," or using what is called "crack."

I Brought Horror into My Parents' Home

Between ages twenty-one and twenty-seven I passed through seven rehab programs and several sober living environments. Searching for relief from my addiction, I tried hypnotism, acupuncture, antidepressants, psychiatry, and everything modern and alternative medicine and psychology had to offer. I spent all my time seeking my poison or searching for the antidote. I wanted relief, but I didn't want to stop.

Addiction is a funny thing. It does a vicious turn on you, a complete 180 degrees. Something that can at first make you feel so good begins to cause you such pain. For the first three years when I was snorting the powder, I suffered a lot of nose bleeds. Then after four additional years of smoking crack, I was fifty pounds underweight, with burn marks and blisters from the hot pipe—in my mouth and on my lips and fingers.

I was living a shallow, dead existence. When I wasn't asleep, I was high. The "yets" started happening. I relied on my parents to bail me out of trouble financially, but I wasn't able to show up in court to deal with my DUIs or convictions for driving on a suspended license, and I couldn't perform my early morning community service after being up all night. I was going to jail because I couldn't do life.

Yet even though I brought horror into my parents' home— calling them from jails and hospitals, robbing them of their money, security, and peace—they never gave up hope in me. While I never worked the twelve steps or got a sponsor— because I wasn't ready to face the things I'd done and the people I'd hurt—my parents talked to priests, directors of rehab centers, and people at Al-Anon meetings, all of whom said the same thing: unless they kicked me out, I wouldn't recover.

My parents did ask me to leave their home a few times, but I returned almost immediately with a well-conceived sob story. I would promise them the world, show them the best of intentions, offer a good plan, and give them the consolation and comfort they needed to let me in. Then the next day, my words would fly out the window. My parents didn't believe that kicking me out of the house was the answer anyway. Their love remained as thick as their denial.

As my addiction progressed, I could no longer hold a job for even a few days. I faded to skin and bones and became paranoid, refusing to leave the house except to purchase more drugs. In my deranged mental state, I thought that several drug dealers were out to kill me—and they probably were. I was going to the projects daily, entering places that used to make me shudder when I glanced at them from the freeway. I was getting beat up, held up, shot at, and carjacked; and, still, I kept going back. The devil wanted me dead.

I Felt They Would Take Me Somewhere and Shoot Me

One cold and drizzly October night, around two in the morning, I drove my dad's Cadillac into the projects. Most nights, dozens of people would walk up and down the street that I frequented, but this night was rare. No one was out but one man, standing under a single street light. I bought a small amount of dope from him and then drove away, feeling wary. He looked more like a user than a dealer. After pulling over, I tested the drug to make sure it was real, as I always did before purchasing from someone I didn't know.

He walked back over to the car, and I asked for more. I saw him reach down into his sock. But what I thought was his holding place for dope was his holster for a gun. He pulled out the weapon and aimed it at my head, then ordered me to unlock the door, shut off the car, and give him the keys. I froze, contemplating whether to accelerate away from him or do as he said. Realizing that my foot wasn't faster than his finger, I shut the car off and unlocked the door.

Out of the darkness appeared a woman at the window of my passenger side. She and the man were going to get into the car on either side of me. I felt they would take me some-where and shoot me, so I stalled, sitting in the driver's seat with the gun on me, not resisting, not complying, just trying to buy time.

The man didn't seem at all nervous or agitated, but ap-peared eerily calm and cold. He then changed his demand from moving me to the middle of the car seat to telling me to exit the car. He wanted more money, and I told him all I had was twenty dollars. He insisted I had more and made me strip my clothes off in the middle of the street.

There I stood, totally naked, with a .357 pointed at my head. An extremely sick feeling washed over me, as I waited for something to happen. "It will be horrible for my parents to find out that I died this way," I thought.

Then, while his accomplice began ransacking the car, look-ing for anything of value, he opened the trunk of the car, and a new fear seized me. "He is planning on putting my dead body in the trunk." All the blood rushed out of my head, and a new surge of paralyzing nausea pooled in my stomach, then overwhelmed my whole body. "This is my last few seconds," I thought, as I waited for a bullet to hit me. "It's gonna hurt when I get shot. My parents will be destroyed." I didn't say anything but continued to make eye contact with the man. See-ing nothing in the trunk, he wiped his fingerprints off my keys and keychain and dropped them on the ground; then he and his accomplice vanished.

As I drove away from the scene, what most upset me—besides the humiliation I suffered—was the fact that the man had taken my drug money. Now I had neither drugs nor the money to buy them. I wanted to run him over with my car but somehow continued to steer toward home. Terrifying as that episode was, it wasn't enough to deter me. It simply made me more street-wise.

"That's Enough. It's a Murder Rap."

On another night, a warm summer night outlined by a full moon, I went into the projects again around 10:00 p.m.—this time on foot, with only five dollars to spend. Having lost my license in a DUI, I had taken the bus to get there. Any person not suffering from my compulsion would never dream of entering this part of town. In my youth, grownups had told me about it. Murders were committed there weekly, alongside other crimes of horror. For most of my life, I had shuddered as I passed by the plain, nondescript sets of block housing. Now I'd been going there daily for several years. I knew everyone who lived there and had never had any serious problems with the twenty or so people usually milling about. But this night was different.

I walked into the building's central cement courtyard, which was covered with a chaotic scene of at least a hundred people, with barbecuing, music, dancing, madness, buying, selling, cars ripping through, rap music pounding, men drinking, and women strewn on every balcony. A ten-year-old boy immediately ran up to me at the entrance with a handful of crack. I looked at him and thought, "I'm not buying from a baby," and walked away from the kid. But then I had second thoughts. I turned back around to look for him when I heard laughing from teenage girls on the balcony: "Ah, he's scared to come in here!" one of them called out.

Then my pride kicked in. "Can't handle it?" So I turned around, walked right up to a group of men I hadn't met before (whom I profiled to be drug dealers), and said, "Give me a twenty," which means, "I want twenty dollars worth of crack."

Something about my bold approach and my look, along with my nice jacket and glasses, took them aback. I was immediately labeled.

One replied, "I ain't got no crack here, cop." And another added, "You'd better get the f--- out of here and tell your narc buddies around the corner to get on." Then someone hit me in the head from behind. From there ensued a vicious, frenzied beating as a group of eight or ten men punched me, kicked me, stomped on me, and clubbed me with baseball bats.

As the blows kept coming, severe pain turned into a numb, dull, hollow pressure that came with each hit. The body can only take so much. Doing my best to cover my head, I lay on the ground, crying out in loud, painful, muffled screams.

Women on the balconies wailed excitedly with panic in their voices: "No, he's not a cop! We know him!" But the men weren't listening. A mob mentality had seized them. All they knew was that cop meant prison.

While on the verge of losing consciousness, I heard a voice in the background saying, "That's enough. It's a murder rap," which means, "If you continue, he'll die." When he spoke, they all retreated. None of them wanted to get caught killing a police officer. That man saved my life; I'm sure of it.

As I staggered to my feet, I felt on the verge of passing out. A large ring of people surrounded me—not a happy bunch. They were there to see someone get hurt. I wanted to run, but I couldn't get my feet to move. Weak and dizzy, I stumbled a few feet in the direction of the street. A voice angrily ordered me to hurry up, and then I heard a bullet whiz by my head. That woke up my senses. I knew I had to get out of there quickly. In a surge of fear, I started running, and as I was about to exit the compound, a man ran up to me to steal the jacket right off my back. Ready to fight, I soon realized that the only way I was going to leave alive was to give it to him. The others had long since taken my wallet and keys.

After I relinquished my brand-new leather jacket to the opportunist, I made my way to the nearest pay phone. As I tried to reach for the receiver, I couldn't move my arm. My collar bone had been crushed. Using my other arm, I made a phone call to my dad. He could tell by the sound of my voice that something was terribly wrong.

When he picked me up he took me directly to the hospital, where I received numerous stitches to my face and head. My father later told my mom that when he saw me, he almost cried. I've only seen my father cry once in my life. I had been a bloody mess, with lacerations, scrapes, and cuts covering my face, hands, and head. I put my parents through hell.

With Each Passing Day, the Peace Inside Me Increased

My father is a man of great faith who has suffered immensely. He grew up poor, and his father died when he was a teenager. As a fairly young man, he lost his first wife and four children in a tragic house fire that the San Francisco Fire Department still remembers as the worst they've encountered in their history. My father lost his sister to a heartbreaking death, not to mention the many years of trouble he endured from my addiction. Despite all of this, he clung to his faith, surviving storm after storm because of his profound trust in God.

One day as he sat in church praying about my circumstances, lest he lose his only son to a deadly spiritual malady, he received an internal message: "Take your son to Medjugorje." My family knew of Medjugorje because my mother had scoured through books on the subject and read Mary's monthly messages to us ever since my sister and I were very young.

A friend of our family named Donna had even visited our home after going on a pilgrimage there in order to share stories from her trip. Her experiences included such miraculous events as seeing the links of rosaries turn a golden color, having vivid visions of the devil and the Mother of God, and witnessing the miracle of the sun (the ability to stare at the sun for long stretches of time without any ill effects, as it spins in the sky). As I listened, I picked apart her stories bit by bit until nothing credible remained in them. Yet nine years later, when my father came home from church and asked me if I would go with him on a pilgrimage to Medjugorje, I agreed, in desperation, hoping it would be my deliverance.

The night before we left, my mother brought me my rosary, one that my aunt in Ireland had sent me for my Confirmation when I was twelve. It had been lying untouched in a box for years. "Take this with you," she said, "and I bet its links are going to turn gold."

She even went so far as to have me look at the links and tell her what color they were. "They're silver," I remarked skeptically.

When I arrived in Medjugorje, I experienced, for the very first time in my life, a true sense of peace. I could pray smoothly and tirelessly, even though I had never before been able to quiet my mind or clear my head, much less pray through my racing thoughts. Not only that, but from the moment we departed from the United States, I suffered no ill effects of withdrawal; whereas, normally, if I abruptly stopped drinking or taking drugs, I passed through a miserable period of heavy detoxification with notable agitation and excessive sleep. With no stress or obsessive cravings for drugs and alcohol, I felt like a different person—a person who could see that life was worth living after all.

Our first day there, my father and I climbed up Apparition Hill while praying the rosary. Unconcerned with anything but the present moment, I prayed with my heart, my whole heart, for the first time. With an earnest longing, I prayed to Mary and Jesus for freedom from my addiction.

The second day, we climbed up Cross Mountain. It took at least an hour for us to ascend the rocky terrain, marked by the Stations of the Cross; and when we arrived at the top, I went off on my own to be alone and look out at the beautiful panoramic view. I could see miles of fields and mountains extending away from me, with smatterings of houses huddled in patches. Sitting down in the middle of a small, quiet meadow strewn with reddish-brown, jagged rocks—hallmarks of the Medjugorje landscape—I took out my rosary. Hail Mary after Hail Mary passed effortlessly as my fingers traveled along the beads, and I thought of Donna's account of staring at the sun as it spun in the sky. Every so often, I looked up and tried to stare at it, but my eyes watered and closed, protecting themselves against the bright glare.

As I neared the end of the prayers, I balled the rosary into my hand, closing my fingers around it tightly, unconsciously desiring to hold onto this new treasure of peace I had found. When I opened my hand and looked down, my heart jumped with astonishment. The entire rosary began to glow and glisten bright gold. I sat and stared at it for quite a while, fixated with awe. Then, slowly, the glow dissipated, and as I examined my rosary closely, I saw that the links between the beads had turned a yellowish color, but only between the Hail Mary beads and not the Our Father beads. A great sense of comfort welled up in me, and my eyes filled with tears. I felt special. In that moment my perception of humanity's relationship with

God changed. In the palm of my hand, I had seen that the Creator's love was deeply personal.

During the rest of the trip, the gold color of the metal links on my rosary became deeper, richer, and brighter; and with each passing day, the peace inside me increased. By the end of the week, my rosary chain looked like twenty-four carat gold.

About four days into the pilgrimage, I was again trying to look at the sun. At midday, with the sun at its unbearable brightest, I glanced upward. At first, I didn't trust what was happening: I was staring directly at the sun, which was dancing, spinning, and pulsating in the sky. As if to test the miracle, I continued to stare at it as long as I wished, and whenever I looked away, I saw no black sun spots. In fact, everything appeared to me as though blanketed with sparkling golden dust.

Nine years earlier, when Donna had shared her tale of seeing the sun spin and her rosary turn gold, I'd thought to myself, "Sun spinning? I guess you took too much acid in school. Rosaries turning gold? Yeah, right. God's really that materialistic. And seeing visions! That's hysteria."

Two of the miracles I had doubted the most were the first two things God showed me, and in exceptionally beautifully ways, as if to say, "Why do you question these small things?"

Medjugorje Was the Safest, Most Peaceful Place on Earth

Yet God didn't stop there with giving me proof of his presence and attention. Over the next few hours, God tried to instill more trust and understanding in me, and it wasn't an easy teaching. His lesson began that night, as I woke up to the sound of my dad stirring. "What are you doing?" I asked him.

"I'm going for a walk."

"Now? What time is it?"

"It's around 2:00 a.m."

I felt as though I should go with him, but something prevented me from doing so. My dad reassured me that he'd be fine and promised to be back by 7:00 a.m., in time for breakfast, so I went back to sleep. At 7:00 a.m. the next morning, he was nowhere to be found, and no one at the hotel had seen him that morning either.

I grew concerned and set out looking for him. I made the half-mile journey from our hotel to St. James Church and back, hoping to see him along the way. After searching for half an hour, I returned to find he still hadn't come back. Time went on, and I became increasingly concerned, fearing the worst. Not fully understanding where I was in the world—Medjugorje being perhaps the safest, most peaceful place on earth—I wondered if my father had fallen victim to a violent attack during the night.

By 10:00 a.m., I was preparing myself to call my mother and tell her some very bad news. My dad had been gone eight hours, and I thought he was dead. I had gone back and forth from the hotel to the church at least five times, and I had most of our group out looking for him. I finally sat down, in despair, in front of the church. A couple of minutes later, a little Irish priest came up to me and asked, "Is everything all right?"

I could tell he was in a rush, so I said, "Well, not really."

"Whatever is going on with you," he responded, "I'll offer Mass for you today."

Wayne Weible, a popular author on the subject of Medjugorje, was speaking in the outdoor arena behind the church, and I sat down with our group, scanning the crowd, desperately looking for my father. At one point, my eyes looked up at

Cross Mountain in the background, and I said silently, "God, where is he?"

I received an interior message that replied, "He's okay. He's with us." A gentle calm swept over me, and I sensed that my father was praying next to the cross on top of the mountain. In my mind's eye, I saw him stand up and wave his arms, and I could hear him saying, "It's okay, Mike. I'm okay." Completely set at peace by this experience, I knew at that moment that he was just fine.

After the talk, I entered the church for Mass, and the little Irish priest was the celebrant. Being such a doubting Thomas, I stopped trusting the assurance God had given me. As I was praying during the Mass, tense and worried, my father suddenly arrived and sat next to me. Feeling wildly overjoyed and absolutely furious at the same time, I waited until after Mass to let him have it. The minute we stepped outside the church, I told him exactly what he had put me through. He apologized, saying he had realized that I would be worried, but he knew he was called to be on top of the mountain. Then he laughed a little and said, "Now you've gotten a little glimpse of what your mother and I go through every night." I winced.

Then we started comparing stories. He told me that he had indeed been praying next to the cross. At the very same time, around 11:00 a.m., when I had sensed he was okay, he had been talking to me silently from his soul, reassuring me, saying the same words I had heard, "It's okay, Mike. I'm okay." And, he had felt a strange urge to stand up and wave his arms, but didn't.

Toward the very end of the trip, I became anxious again, and my craving for drugs returned. As we traveled back to the States through Germany, I felt spiritually attacked. I later learned, by speaking with others who had been to Medjugorje, that many people feel bombarded with negativity upon leaving that holy place. My peace was being stripped away, and my father was experiencing something similar. We were sensing the glaring contrast between good and evil, and the evil forces seemed directly targeted at us. By the time our plane landed in San Francisco, I had already planned to meet my drug dealer that night.

The Blessed Mother Intervened, So I Could Live

I have come to understand that a drug addict is not fully responsible for his or her addiction. It is true that I made the choice to ingest substances in the first place, and that was deadly wrong—but I had little control over what happened next. Just as the Church has its sacraments, and Jesus is fully present in them—particularly in the form of the Host at Mass— I believe that the devil is present in drugs, his medium for the ruin of many souls on earth.

Before Medjugorje, my prayers consisted only of brief cries of despair: "God, please help me! I can't continue living like this!" I felt ashamed to pray and had a poor spiritual connection with God. After I returned, when I wasn't on drugs, I was saying the rosary. Newly aware of the benefits and the graces I could receive while praying, I didn't want to give them up. For the very first time, I had hope, yet my drug-seeking behavior changed little.

One night as I was standing on a street corner, prepared to buy a large quantity of crack, an unfamiliar car approached me. I had four hundred dollars in my jacket sleeve and some coins, keys, a twenty, and my rosary in my pockets. A man whom I'd never seen before reached his head out of the car window and asked what I needed. Responding with suspicion, I told him I only needed a "twenty."

The car pulled around the corner, and out came three men. One pulled out a revolver and shoved it at my belly. As the other two grabbed each of my arms, the first man told me to give him the money. I offered him the twenty dollars in my pocket, and then he ordered me to give him the jacket. Although terrified, I refused, because I knew they would find my drug money. In my insanity, I preferred to risk getting shot than to give up my supply. While I was shoving back and forth with the two men on either side of me, the man with the gun began angrily rifling through my pockets. Finding the rosary beads, he pulled them out and held them up in front of his face. The four of us suddenly froze, staring at the beads dangling from his closed fist.

It took me a second to realize that all three of the men were in some kind of suspended animation. Frozen in a supernatural, inexplicable way, with their eyes fixated on the rosary, they were no longer aware of my presence. I saw an opportunity to escape. Carefully freeing myself from their grip, I backed away without fully understanding what was going on. Then I started to run, briefly glancing back at the frozen men as I darted around the corner.

For a moment, I wanted to return to snatch my precious treasure from the man's suspended grip, but common sense and fear overrode that thought. I entered a nearby bar and, with a trembling hand, picked up the telephone to call a cab. As I kept an eye on the bar's western-style, swinging front doors, the three heads of the men suddenly popped in. My heart pounded with fear. All three men stared right at me with looks of confusion and amazement. Then they looked at each other and disappeared. As the swinging doors settled into stillness, so did my heart. I believe I was going to die that day, and the Blessed Mother, through the power of Christ's mercy, intervened so I could live.

For the next several days, my mother came to me and asked to see my rosary. "I'll show it to you later," I responded. I put her off for as long as I could until she finally realized I had lost it. Finally, I confessed, but said I didn't know where it had gone. She went into her room and reappeared with the rosary I had brought back as a gift to her from Medjugorje. I protested, but she insisted. That night, I slept with my new rosary next to my pillow, and by morning, its chain links had turned a gold color, as well. I felt deeply consoled and yet emotionally torn. God and the Blessed Mother were again showing me their great love, but I wasn't living up to their gift.

I Was Looking at Mary, the Mother of God

I entered yet another treatment center, and that failed, or I failed it. My using grew uglier, as I elongated a trail of destruction in my family, like a runaway train crashing recklessly into cherished property. My parents continued to bail me out of jail until I got a DUI and didn't go to DUI school, do community service, go to court, or pay my fine. When the police put a warrant out for my arrest and subsequently picked me up, my parents preferred to leave me in the county jail, because there, at least, they knew I was safe.

Less than a year after my first trip to Medjugorje, I told my family that all of us needed to go there. I wanted to get back the peace I had squandered and lost. My family agreed to go, in the hope that I would receive a healing from my addiction; so together, along with family friends, we traveled across the world to Bosnia and Herzegovina. There in Medjugorje, I roomed with a friend named Matthew, who hoped and prayed that the pilgrimage would result in a miraculous healing for his brother, Patrick, a young man also suffering from addiction.

Once again, I arrived with no drugs, no discomfort, no depression—not a single symptom of withdrawal. Once again, I felt happy and at peace. During our stay, Matthew and I spent a long evening that turned into night, talking about our lives. As we walked along a dark road from the center of town toward our bed-and-breakfast, he opened up to me about his pain over his brother Patrick's addiction. It was tearing his family apart, and he struggled to understand the nature and lure of his affliction. Our discussion grew emotionally intense, and at one point, after sharing hours of stories and perspectives, I experienced a moment of clarity. I realized that my addiction was a ploy of the devil to keep me trapped and confused in darkness, far from the light of God and unable to live as he made me.

Shortly after this revelation, as we walked on in the dark night and were about to make a right turn toward the bed-and-breakfast, Matthew said to me suddenly, "What's that?" I looked up to see a brilliantly illuminated figure about fifty feet in front of us and off to the right. It was standing ten feet tall and eight or ten feet off of the ground—low enough to be partially obstructed by bushes and high enough to be seen above the trees. It glowed with an otherworldly intensity and quality of light that defied the laws of physics: although its brightness could have lit up an entire stadium, it shed no light on its surroundings, nor did it hurt our eyes. The illumination appeared in the shape of Mary on the Miraculous Medal—the image that God gave to St. Catherine Labouré in 1830, with Mary's arms extended slightly away from her sides and her palms titled upward, in a gesture of offering grace to the world.

Not saying a word, Matthew and I instinctively started moving toward the luminous figure. In an attempt to take a side trail directly toward it, we got tangled in the landscape of thorn bushes, trees, and stone walls, so we continued along the main road, which led uphill. But as we pursued the light, it moved farther away. We quickened our pace, watching it slip behind trees and then reappear again. After following it for about a city block, we darted into an open, grassy field, and there we saw the spectacular figure in full view. It stopped directly in front of us, and we immediately fell to our knees, overwhelmed.

I was looking at Mary, the Mother of God, and I knew it. Tears ran down my face, as I felt the love that was emanating from her pierce through my being. Infused with wonder and joy, feeling no shock or fear, we continued kneeling, hoping to gaze at her for hours. After a couple of minutes passed, I asked her, "Blessed Mother, may we come forward?" No reply. Another minute passed, and I asked, "What do you want of us?"

Without saying anything, she started to move again, pulling away and up the hill, this time moving faster than before. We sprang to our feet and into a sprint, pursuing her excitedly up the main road. After chasing her a few hundred yards, we attempted to take a shortcut by entering the front gates of a newly constructed building at the top of the hill. Out of breath and exhilarated, we found ourselves within the fenced-in courtyard of a property that looked to me much like a California winery. Not wanting to lose sight of her, I ran up the side of a six-foot-high mound of dirt and peered over the fence to see her bright figure, several hundred yards away, move toward the lower side of Cross Mountain and come to rest there. Then in the blink of an eye, she vanished from the hillside.

Thrilled, yet confused, and a half-mile off course, Matthew and I looked at each other in wide-eyed amazement. "What just happened? What does it all mean?" we asked. In a daze, we wandered back to the bed-and-breakfast and almost woke up our friends and family in order to share our excitement, but decided to wait until morning. We talked into the night, stirring up more questions than answers, and finally fell asleep as the sun rose over Cross Mountain.

Mary Had Said Everything to Me, Without Saying Anything at All

Very early the next morning, at around 6:00 a.m., my mother peeked into Matthew's and my room and said, "Come on, get up, time for breakfast, and then we're going to see the house of the drug addicts." When we had arrived in Medjugorje, she had heard about a community for recovering drug addicts and wayward young men, and she wanted to make sure I visited it.

I hadn't ever heard of this place, and after only a couple hours of sleep, I had no desire to see it, or anything for that matter. "I'm tired," I moaned. "We've been up all night." She pleaded with me to get up, so I complied, looking enviously at my friend on the other side of the room.

He peered at me through one eye, as if to say, "Hee, hee, I'm not going," and pulled the covers over his head.

I dragged myself out of bed, ate breakfast, and joined about one hundred people who were gathering outside, ready to walk to the community. Too tired to share the experience of the night before, I began walking up the hill in silence, retracing the night's events in my mind. As we turned to enter the gates of the community, I saw that I was entering a place that looked like a California winery. "A 'winery'?! The 'winery' is the house for recovering drug addicts! This is exactly where the Blessed Mother led us!" She had said everything to me, without saying anything at all.

I was standing at the entrance of the property called Comunitá Cenacolo, a home for young men with addiction problems. It was created by the prayers and tireless work of a joyful, charismatic Italian nun named Sr. Elvira Petrozzi, who has founded many such homes throughout the world. Bursting with excitement, I told my mom that I would be right back. I was going to run back to wake up Matthew and tell him of my discovery. But my mother grabbed my arm and began to cry, pleading with me to stay so that I wouldn't miss the experience.

So I walked into a chapel full of attentive pilgrims and half-listened as two young Italian men, who had come to Comunitá Cenacolo in the same desperate condition I was currently in, began to share their life stories of drug use and recovery. As I sat, distracted by my burning desire to share what had happened with Matthew, I studied and admired a beautiful fifteen-by ten-foot icon behind the two men speaking, which depicted the resurrected Jesus pulling Adam and Eve from their underground tombs. I understood, at that moment, that the Lord had the power to pull me from my dark, internal dwelling. As my eyes followed the sacred contours of the icon, the thought struck me that I was truly in the right place. Just then, unexpectedly, the side door opened, and Matthew walked into the room. We looked at each other with a knowing glance. Later, he told me that, despite his overwhelming desire to sleep in, something made him get up and join us.

After the talk, as we were walking out of the building, my mother came to me with tears in her eyes and said, "Patrick needs to come here." We both knew what she meant. She meant that I, too, needed to live there, but her fear of my rejection kept her from voicing my name. I immediately broke into tears and said, "I know." But my will wasn't yet united with my words.

I wandered through my successive days in Medjugorje with a sweet, consoling angel on one shoulder and a smooth-talking, vociferous demon on the other. The angel was whispering, "Life is beautiful. God loves you. You can be free from addiction and lead a normal life."

The demon was countering, "Drugs make you comfortable. That's all you know, that's all you have left. You can have the best of both worlds. You can learn how to control your using, still live a good life, and feel the peace of God."

I left Medjugorje with enough money to use again and did so within a couple of days.

My Doubts Had Taken the Miracle Away

When I got home, I could stare at the sun for an hour straight. Then the doubts came. I began to dissect every miracle I'd witnessed in Medjugorje. I convinced myself that the links on my rosary had turned a gold color because of a chemical reaction: "The different atmosphere there in Medjugorje must have oxidized the metal when combined with the moisture in my hand." I ignored the fact that my other rosary had turned gold in the air at home, without the benefit of my sweaty palm. I also convinced myself that I had always been able to stare straight into the sun. "I just never attempted it because people warned me against going blind. Maybe the atmosphere in Medjugorje has more ozone in it, which protects the eyes."

When these thoughts came, suddenly I couldn't stare at the sun any longer. Then I knew I'd been privy to a miracle, because my doubts had taken it away. After that, if I looked at the sun for more than a few seconds, my eyes teared immediately, I saw purple spots, and I had to look down. The one thing I never doubted or denied, though, was that night of seeing Mary.

My family wanted to believe I was miraculously healed of my addiction in Medjugorje because they had such great faith. But I didn't need to simply stop using drugs; I needed to make up for a life of bad decisions, a life in which I never really consciously participated. I was twenty-seven years old, unmotivated, unskilled, and without a single goal. "If I were to stop drugs," I wondered, "then what?" Not only did I need to learn the tasks of sobriety, I was missing something that was second nature to people. I didn't know how to live.

Making matters worse, the devil seemed to be in a panic to destroy me. Now that I had hope and the understanding that God wanted me to enter a recovery community, a battle had ended. But the war had just begun. My addiction increased ten-fold. My cravings became insatiable. For two months, I used large amounts of crack during all my waking hours and looked like a walking skeleton, with shifty, blood-shot eyes and pale skin covering my hollow insides.

I Was Willing to Try to Embrace Another Way

One day after taking a hit of crack in my parents' bathroom, I walked into the kitchen where my father was sorting through paperwork, and he said, "You know, when are you going to give that place in Florida a call?"

I looked at him, puzzled. "What place in Florida?" He proceeded to tell me about a house in North America connected with the Cenacolo program in Medjugorje. It was the only Cenacolo house in the United States and the traditional vehicle through which Americans entered the community.

Normally, if such a suggestion were made to me, I would have said, "Yeah, yeah," with absolutely no intention of acting on it. But I asked my father for the Florida community's phone number and then made the phone call, still high. The community asked me to travel there within the next two weeks, and I agreed—a completely unusual reaction on my part, because I had always tried to avoid the inevitable by extending the timeline of my recovery; but part of me felt so disgusted with my life that I was willing to try to embrace another way.

I yo-yoed in and out of the Florida community three times, making various excuses for why I had to leave. My most famous one was a complete, manipulative lie: "Mom, Dad, I've gotten a girl from one of the rehab centers pregnant, and I need to go home to take care of the child."

During my third stay, Matthew's brother Patrick also entered the community, and over the next few months we developed a friendship. Together we had to sacrifice almost everything. We could own nothing. We had no music, television, cigarettes, girls, newspapers, or contact with the outside world. Our days consisted primarily of work and prayer. Eventually, Patrick was sent to the house in Medjugorje, and a couple of months later, feeling disgruntled and abandoned, I accomplished my third escape.

Christianne Captivated Me

Shortly after I returned to my parents' home, I met Matthew and Patrick's sister, Christianne. As I sat in Patrick's coffee shop in San Francisco (which his family was managing in his absence), I struck up my first conversation with her. In an instant, she captivated me. I sensed she was someone special, someone who didn't just stumble through life, someone who had known God for a long time. We discussed Medjugorje, our faith, and our lives. The ease and comfort with which I could speak to her about spiritual things gave me a door to an entirely new experience of connecting with another human being.

As much as I felt drawn to her, marriage strayed far from my radar. My life was still a catastrophe.

Shortly after that, I met Christianne again at a prayer gathering my parents held at our home every Monday night. After another enjoyable conversation, this time on my parents' moonlit front porch, she told me she was going to leave the next day to visit Patrick in Medjugorje. We said our secretly reluctant goodbyes, and then, with determination, I turned around and walked back inside to tell my mother I had made up my mind to live in the rehabilitation community. She looked overjoyed.

Assuming I would have to go back to the community in Florida, I called to see if I could return, but the staff told me to call every morning for a month just after waking up, to show my commitment and interest. At the end of the month, they informed me that they had spoken to Sister Elvira in Italy, who said that if I wanted to return, I had to return to the community in Medjugorje. A shower of relief came over me because I couldn't imagine returning to Florida after my three escapes, and although Medjugorje was five times as far away, it was where I felt most at home.

The next time I saw Christianne, she was driving me to the airport for my departure to Medjugorje, accompanied by Matthew and my sister in the backseat. Together, the four of us had lunch at the airport, and then I boarded a plane with my sister, who had seized the opportunity to travel again to Medjugorje. As the plane left the ground, I said to her, "I know this is crazy, but I think I'm going to marry Christianne."

Ever fearless in speaking her mind, my sister responded, "What? What the heck are you talking about?"

"I can't explain it," I told her, "but I got this feeling. I wasn't even thinking of marriage until just now. But I'm asking you, please, when you get back home from Medjugorje, tell Christianne I want to marry her." I figured I would throw caution to the wind. I wouldn't see Christianne for another three years, so what did I have to lose?

My sister said, "No way. You're crazy. I'm not doing that." But I convinced her that she had to, so she begrudgingly agreed.

For the next three years, every time I prayed the rosary and every time I sat in adoration of the Blessed Sacrament, I said, "This is my desire, God, to marry Christianne, but I'm going to leave my future in your hands."

When my sister returned home from Medjugorje, Christianne picked her up from the airport with Matthew's girlfriend, Janet, also in the car. After engaging in small talk about the trip, my sister said to Christianne, "I have something really weird to tell you."

"What?" Christianne asked.

"I can't believe I'm even going to say this, but my brother thinks he's going to marry you."

Christianne and Janet burst out laughing because Christianne had been talking to Janet about me since I had left, saying, "So he's got a little crack problem. He's cute. I like him. But what am I supposed to do? Wait three years?"

Three and a half years later we were married.

"Our Lady Has Protected You Your Whole Life"

I prayed for four primary things when I lived in the Cenacolo community: to be free from drugs, to spend personal time with Sr. Elvira, to learn how to paint icons, and to have a relationship with Christianne, all the while never knowing what was in her heart.

Communitá Cenacolo was not a drug rehabilitation center, but a school of life. Prayer was an essential, vital part of each day. During my first two years there, by obediently following the guidelines of the community, I learned to change my ways of acting, reacting, and thinking in order to be free from addiction. I had to face many challenges and pass through many tunnels of growth, healing, and rapid change. I learned to rely on God for everything and began to realize that he could take care of me far better than I would ever be able to take care of myself. Over time, I became an entirely different man.

By living in a monastic way, I made many true, lasting friendships; my body healed; and I learned the basic skills of building, farming, gardening, and most importantly, perseverance through hardship with prayer—the antidote to falling into detrimental behaviors. After two years of difficult manual labor, God finally answered one of my special intentions: on the Feast of the Assumption of Mary, Sr. Elvira asked me to take a walk with her—a rare opportunity due to her busy schedule.

With more than fifty houses and thousands of young men and women throughout the world clamoring for solitary time with her, I felt privileged and elated to speak with this holy nun who spends hours of her time in prayer and exudes the joy and wisdom of the Spirit. As we walked through the grounds of the community, I shared my life story with her, ending with my profound spiritual experiences in Medjugorje, which had led me to Cenacolo. After listening intently, she said, "Our Lady has protected you your whole life." Then I took the opportunity to tell her of my burning desire to learn iconography. With eyes that smiled, she said, "You will begin to paint tomorrow."

I was immediately relocated to a different house where I began my instructions from an Italian man who had learned to "write" icons from a nun in Jerusalem twelve years earlier. An iconographer is said to "write," rather than paint, an icon because each picture tells a story full of meaning. My instructor expressed his enthusiasm over my aptitude toward iconography, and as I studied under him, I discovered a fresh outlook on life. The art of writing icons gave me purpose and fulfillment. The paintbrush led me to self-forgiveness and newfound self-respect and energy that I didn't know I had.

I Learned How to Live

After writing icons for nearly a year, Sr. Elvira asked me if I was ready to visit home. The community suggested that if, after a ten-day leave, I felt I was ready to exit the community, I should slowly adapt to the outside world by leaving via the Florida community, where I could live with other men transitioning out of the community. I ignored their advice and went straight back to San Francisco, where my horror story had been written.

Moving out of a rehabilitation community into an independent life is like handing a toddler car keys. Surrounded by old temptations and reemerging familiar thoughts, I adjusted, with difficulty, to having a free will without the protection and structure of a community. But through it all, I never dove into a full relapse, and God, in his unwavering mercy, answered another of my prayers. I was able to spend most of my time with Christianne, and the instant love and attraction we felt for each other was overpowering. Two months after I returned to San Francisco, we were engaged.

Seven months later, and just two months before the wedding, I finally attended an Alcoholics Anonymous meeting after shedding my excuses that I had been good for so long, said so many prayers, and lived such a clean life that I was over my addiction. In the Cenacolo Community, I learned how to live; I learned discipline and perseverance; but I needed a program of spiritual substance to keep myself in check. Now I feel that my attendance at AA meetings will be lifelong, not because I fear I will use drugs, but because the gatherings help me to detach from the business of life. They ground me, remind me of my past, and keep me focused on God—on what is most important.

Christianne and I were married in Italy. We spent our honeymoon in Medjugorje. Patrick was my best man. He, too, had gotten married, and his wife joined us, along with many of our family members. To return to Medjugorje with our wives, our health, and our sanity felt to us like an unparalleled grace.

On my last day in Medjugorje, as I stood on top of Cross Mountain, grateful to be alive, to be in love, to be happy, I reflected back upon the moment when I ran up the hill after the shining figure of Our Lady, not knowing where she was leading me or why. Although it became clear what she wanted of me, the magnitude of her intervention from heaven never struck me until I was able to live the fruits of my experience in community. I was led, by her hand, to the middle of the Cenacolo courtyard for the salvation of my soul. I didn't appreciate the gravity of that moment then. I could say what had happened and understand it to an extent, but to truly realize how much I was protected and loved, I'm not sure I can fully grasp that even now.

Dear children, as I look at you, my heart seizes with pain. Where are you going my children? Have you sunk so deeply into sin that you do not know how to stop yourselves? You justify yourselves with sin and live according to it. Kneel down beneath the Cross and look at my Son. He conquered sin and died so that you, my children, may live. Permit me to help you not to die but to live with my Son forever. Thank you!

—Mary's message of October 2, 2009, from www.Medjugorje.org

For Prayerful Reflection

In order to heal from his past and to contend with the temptations of his addiction, Michael spent three years in the Cenacolo community. There his heart could be free to empty itself of past years, pour out prayers of repentance, and humbly begin anew. Across the world and across time, such prayers of soul-searching honesty have changed the course of history, one life at a time.

> Have mercy on me, God, in your goodness; in your
>   abundant compassion blot out my offense.
> Wash away all my guilt; from my sin cleanse me.
> For I know my offense; my sin is always before me.
> Against you alone have I sinned; I have done such
>   evil in your sight that you are just in your
>   sentence, blameless when you condemn.
> True, I was born guilty, a sinner, even as my
>   mother conceived me.
> Still, you insist on sincerity of heart; in my inmost
>   being teach me wisdom.
> Cleanse me with hyssop, that I may be pure; wash
>   me, make me whiter than snow.

Let me hear sounds of joy and gladness; let the
bones you have crushed rejoice.
Turn away your face from my sins; blot out all
my guilt.
A clean heart create for me, God; renew in me a
steadfast spirit.
Do not drive me from your presence, nor take from
me your holy spirit.
Restore my joy in your salvation; sustain in me a
willing spirit.
I will teach the wicked your ways, that sinners may
return to you.
Rescue me from death, God, my saving God, that
my tongue may praise your healing power.
Lord, open my lips; my mouth will proclaim
your praise.
For you do not desire sacrifice; a burnt offering you
would not accept.
My sacrifice, God, is a broken spirit; God, do not
spurn a broken,
humbled heart.

—Psalm 51:3–19

1. Read Psalm 51 again, slowly, meditatively. Which words stand out for you? What are they saying to you?

2. The psalm says, "In your abundant compassion blot out my offense." Do you believe that God blotted out the offenses Michael committed against him? Do you believe that God has blotted out the sins you have confessed to him in the Sacrament of Reconciliation? Are there any sins that still haunt you, even after you confessed them? If so, pray now that God frees you of them and of any guilt, shame, or self-condemnation you carry, once and for all.

3. Michael said that "something mysterious and exciting came with crossing moral boundaries." What began as an exciting journey became an excursion into thickening darkness. Have you ever

started down a road that seemed enticing, or harmless enough, and then found yourself entangled in the devil's trap?

4. Just before leaving Medjugorje on his second pilgrimage, Michael believed the idea that "you can have the best of both worlds. You can learn how to control your using, still live a good life, and feel the peace of God." Rationalizations are little tools with big effects for wide ranges of sin, from "It's okay if I take these pens from work; they don't pay me enough for what I do, anyway," to "Drinking isn't a problem for me because I make sure that when I'm drunk, I take a cab," to "A bunch of cells aren't really a human being, so it's okay to terminate this pregnancy," to "We had to kill people over there because they could hurt us one day." We all rationalize, because we're all human. Spend a moment in prayer and ask God to show you ways you might rationalize certain thoughts or behaviors that could be harmful to you or others.

5. God, through the intercession of Mary, saved Michael on several occasions from death. Have you ever been saved from danger and sensed that God intervened to help you? Take a moment to give God thanks and praise for his care for you.

6. Mary appeared as a bright, otherworldly figure to Michael and Matthew to lead them to the Cenacolo community. Have you ever found yourself in a certain place, at a certain time and thought, "I am supposed to be here right here and right now for a Godly purpose." Did you realize at the time that heaven had arranged for you to be there?

FAITH EXERCISE

Gerald G. May, author of *Addiction and Grace*, says that all of us are addicted to something to varying degrees, whether it be coffee, human praise, sex, or cocaine. St. John of the Cross refers to these addictions as earthly attachments and says that in order to enter fully into God's presence, we must free ourselves of them.

Is there attachment you feel ready to have God break for you? Enter into silent prayer and ask the Lord to help you release your earthly attachment and replace it with a heavenly one.

If an addiction is present, seek help through a rehabilitation center or a 12-step group. You may also want to see a counselor who specializes in addiction. Know that as you go forward in faith, God will smile upon your efforts and reward you.

SIX

CHRISTINE

Mary asks her Son to save a New Ager
from empty promises and a life of deadly sins,
and a miracle occurs.

One night, as I lay in bed at age nine, an agonizing thought
shot through my mind: "I am going to die one day." As much
as I tried to think otherwise, I could not see a way out of it. "If
I'm going to die and be nothing, then why am I here?" I wondered. "What is the point of life?" "Mom! Mom! Come here!"
I shouted. My mother came into my room, and I asked her,
"What will happen when I die?"

She knelt down next to me and said, "It's nothing to worry
about."

"It's nothing to worry about?"

"No. What will happen to you is what will happen to everyone. When we die, we become like the earth."

"Like the earth? Will I know that I'm dead?"

"Probably not, because you won't be around."

"I won't be around?"

"Well, not completely. You'll be like soil in the ground.
You'll either be cremated—that's when your body is burned

and you become like dirt that can help nourish other plants, like trees—or you'll be buried in a box underground."

"Oh," I said, "It's nothing to worry about?" finding her answer horribly worrisome.

"No. It's nothing to worry about. Try not to think about it." Then she got up and said, "Goodnight."

"Try not to think about it," I reminded myself. "It's nothing to worry about."

As she left my room and shut the door, thoughts of dread shot quickly through my mind into my body and left me shivering. "It's nothing to worry about?! . . . But I will be nothing," my thoughts chanted. "There will be no more me to even remember that I once was!" After that, I thought of death often, usually at night in my bed, staring into the darkness of my room, paralyzed with fear.

I Did Not Like Christians

I was raised in a non-religious home, and I did not like Christians. I found them hopelessly misguided by a fairy tale, and at best, annoying. My derogatory view began one Christmas when my parents took me to see a manger scene in the spacious backyard of a home near ours in Berkeley, California. Covering the side of a hill were electrically lit Wise Men and camels and cows and angels and sheep and shepherds and a mom and a dad and a baby. When I looked at the display, I thought it was the most beautiful sight possible. My five-year-old heart felt like it had been transported to heaven, and I thought, "How wonderful it is that my parents have taken me here!" Normally bothered by the cold, my body felt light and expansive inside my winter jacket, and the crisp winter air around me twinkled with joy. I could not take my eyes off the manger scene, and I didn't want to leave. When my parents said it was time to go,

I asked if I could stay longer. I gazed at the lit figures on the hill and they seemed to wink back at me. Not knowing what the scene meant, I asked my dad, "What is this? Who are the people?"

"They're part of a fairy tale about a special baby that was born in a manger, and people came to see him because they thought he was the Son of God," he said.

"It's not real?" I asked.

"No."

"Are you sure?"

"Yes, I'm sure, honey. Now, let's go home." Reluctantly, I took my dad's hand and immediately wondered when I would see it again. I didn't get a chance to return until years later. And when I did, the scene was gone, and so was my wonder.

So I learned, very young, that the Christian story was not real. I was never going to be a Christian—of that much I was sure. In my youth, I also perfected the fine art of worrying and suffered from very low self-esteem and mild depression. I walked with my shoulders hunched, head forward, and eyes lowered, and my heart raced wildly at the thought of speaking up in school or talking to a boy.

I did find joy, though, in ballet and practiced it diligently for years, with such commitment and passion that I ended up dancing professionally with the San Francisco Ballet Company. At age seven, I decided I was going to become a professional ballet dancer, and I became one. I was going to dance until approximately age forty, so I planned. Ballet was my destiny. Nothing else even remotely satisfied me.

Not having been raised in any religion, I didn't know there was a God. For me, ballet quickly became my personal God. At age nineteen, at the height of my dancing abilities and fully in love with my profession, I suffered from back and foot injuries and had three foot operations. This ended my career and took away the only God I ever knew. Devastated, I grew depressed, lost my identity, and lost my hope.

I Ended Up Worse Off Than When I Began

In my sadness, I looked to the New Age movement for answers, and for four years wound through a dizzying maze of practices and therapies. None of them brought me any lasting relief, and I ended up worse off than when I began. My search for "enlightenment" began when I read a book called *Many Lives, Many Masters* by Brian Weiss, who claimed that his hypnotized client told him of her past lives. "I will live again!" I cheered, as my latent fear of becoming dirt when I died disappeared for the very first time. Having opened a door into the New Age, I stepped through it and tried rebirthing, holotropic breathing, the I-Ching, runes, aura readings, visualization, transpersonal psychology, shamanic meditations, numerology, astrology, chakra balancing, energy "healing" through touch, heart-opening rituals, yoga, colon hydrotherapy, yeast-free diets, past-life regression, crystal healing, and psychic readings.

I chanted and sang before Indian gurus, or pictures of them. I sat in a large theater, listening to a female Indian Guru from New York, who I later found out was involved in covering up her torture of her brother, the sexual abuse acts of her predecessor, and her organization's questionable financial practices. I sat on the floor in a lotus position, in front of an Indian Guru named Mata Amritanandamayi, as she rocked rhythmically to bhajans (devotional songs), occasionally reaching her left arm into the sky, with an odd laugh that was anything but contagious. I gathered with others in a home, where we sat and sang, chanted and meditated in front of a large picture of Sai Baba, a guru from India with a very large afro.

I read books by Shakti Gawain, Chris Griscom, Shirley MacLaine, W. Brugh Joy, Ram Dass, Brian Weiss, Louise Hays, Deepak Chopra, and many others. I walked into musty, dimly lit, smoke-filled rooms for tarot card readings. I stayed up late, poring over New Age books to learn about my past life as an Egyptian princess.

Rita Acted Like She Knew the Answers

For a full year, I followed the advice of a psychic named Rita, after receiving an "attunement" session from her during which I fell into a trance-like, peaceful, and pleasurable state. She told me she saw a dove, which meant I was saved. She said that a man would come into my life and pay for everything, and that the words "Matthew Fox" were written over my head. Convinced something supernaturally important had happened to me, I followed her advice to take a semester of graduate classes at Matthew Fox's New Age–based Sophia Center, and moved into the dorms there and into deeper debt and confusion.

I kept thinking I would find the secrets to higher consciousness, that they were right around the corner, but turn after turn led me to more dead ends with more questions.

Rita acted like she knew the answers, so I called her after a semester and asked what to do next. She said I should move from the West Coast to the East Coast, so I did, and moved in with a distant aunt and uncle. Still confused, I called her again. "I'm here. What do I do now?" This time she said I was to take a Harvard summer school class. I got a catalogue, called her back, and said, "Which one?" since none of them appealed to me.

She told me to read her the catalogue of classes, and with partial conviction stated, "You are to take the anthropology class."

I didn't like the class and got nothing out of it, so a couple months later, I phoned her for another appointment to seek further psychic advice. Full of hope, I drove an hour to the next town, parked the car, and lay down on the grass in front of Rita's office, waiting for the time of my appointment to arrive. Without warning or provocation, a burdensome fatigue came over me in an odd, disconcerting way. A fearful question blew through my mind. "Is there something seriously wrong with me?"

When the time for my appointment came, I slowly peeled off the grass and was told by Rita's assistant to wait in the counseling room. I walked into a cold, damp room and flopped into a hardwood chair, like a rag doll with half its stuffing. Twenty minutes passed. Finally Rita entered and sat down across from me. The woman I saw scarcely resembled the woman I remembered. Her eyes darted about through rapidly blinking eyelids, as though focusing on one visual area for too long gave her sharp eye pain; and on top of her slightly plump, seemingly swollen body, her head jerked and wobbled nervously and apparently involuntarily. She seemed unable to sit still without twitching, as though a small animal were scurrying within her. As nicely as I could muster, I said, "I wondered if you were going to get to me. I've been here for quite a while."

"Well, you should have come and gotten me. You should take more responsibility for yourself," she said. The injustice of her telling me to wait, leaving me alone to freeze, and then reprimanding me for it irked me.

Thus the session began with a wrong turn and then began to spin out of control. I asked her for another psychic reading, but she said that counseling was what I needed most. Dissatisfied with her decision, I began to tell her how I wasn't sure what I was supposed to be doing on the East Coast, that I was running out of money, that I didn't learn anything that interested me in the anthropology class, and that I felt ill and depressed much of the time. Rita responded by telling me that I needed to do something to boost my self-esteem—something to make me feel good about myself.

She mentioned that she had just seen one of her clients who had always wanted a nice, new car, and Rita suggested to her that she go ahead and buy one, put it on her credit card, and worry about paying it off later. This suggestion, she said, transformed her client and gave her a new lease on life. "You should do the same," she said.

"I don't want to buy a car," I responded. "I don't need one. My aunt and uncle are lending me theirs."

Upon hearing this, Rita insisted that I look into getting a new car.

"I've never driven a new car and have no desire to," I said. "Besides that, I'm already in debt and don't need to rack up a needless credit card debt as well."

Shaking with irritation and twitching, she countered, "You just don't appreciate yourself enough to do something nice for yourself."

Silently, I thought, "You're nuts, and I never want to speak with you again."

Pulling quickly out of the parking lot, I drove away, watching Rita's office shrink inside my rearview mirror. I had stepped out of our session as though stepping off of a spinning teacup ride and could barely hold my head up or peer through my tears to see the road home. I had been following the advice of a cantankerous looney-toon.

"I'm Not Sure What to Do with My Life"

Stunned into giving up on Rita, but continuing my desperate search for answers, I began to frequent a Hindu/New Age/ Holistic healing center, where I sat down in a weekly circle of silent anonymity among an average of five strangers. One day, the group leader, a short, blond man who looked like John Denver, sat down on his meditation pillow, taking more time than usual to quiet himself—twice restructuring his lotus position with trembling hands. Normally he began our group with chanting, but this time he spoke, struggling to find words that sounded uncharacteristically fragile: "I have unfortunate news to tell you." He paused and took a deep breath. "I have discovered that the gurus I have been following, gurus who claim to be Avatars, incarnations of the divine, have engaged in behaviors that"—he paused, focusing on a spot on the floor in front of him—"that don't honor human dignity." I recalled that the hallway leading to the meditation room had looked bare, but I hadn't noticed why. Now I realized that his string of guru pictures had been taken down.

Becoming hesitantly assertive, he continued, "We must only go to the Source of all Oneness and not use mediators. We can always trust the Source, the One who is Universal Consciousness, who is us, who is All."

"This is deep," I thought to myself.

Needing to explore those depths, I sat, knelt, bowed, and then knelt, stood and bowed and sat, and so on, in a humorless center for Buddhism. And I dutifully arose when it was my turn to visit the Buddhist "master," who sat regally on the floor in a side room with his serious female assistant. "You may kneel before the master and ask him a question," said the assistant.

I recoiled at having to kneel before a stranger, especially one with a look of great self-importance, but purposefully stashing away my first impressions, I said, "I came here to the East Coast because a psychic told me to, and now that I'm here I'm not sure what to do with myself or my life. What is the meaning of life, anyway?"

The master, a tall, white, all-American guy with the look of a quarterback, said in a booming voice, "I cannot answer that. What do you think?"

"I don't know," I said, "What do you think?"

He paused, allowing enough time for an awkward silence then said, "I don't know. What do you think?"

I Felt Sick Inside My Soul

The false New Age promises of healing and enlightenment weren't my only destructive hopes. From an early age, and especially after I lost my dance career, I looked for comfort and happiness in intimate relationships and sank ever deeper into a mire of sin. I had felt so unclean just after I became sexually active, but as I continued with my behavior, that insidious feeling went away.

Sex never attracted me much, though; I simply wanted to be loved and held. I felt temporarily filled with life when I was in a relationship, but when things failed, as they inevitably did, I was left with an even larger empty, dark, and lonely hole within me. When I didn't have a boyfriend, my mind would scramble for comfort and fixate on who might be next. If I couldn't think of someone, I found fleeting satisfaction in pulling out a list of men I had slept with, as though it were a trophy. Life without a boyfriend meant desperate misery, so I would scan rooms, streets, and clubs with a lonely hunger, hoping to find "him."

The New Age movement had fueled my promiscuity by placing no moral values upon sex, and it fostered my despair by providing no means of salvation. That summer on the East Coast, I continued to walk straight into spiritual barbed wire, signing up for more and more New Age workshops, searching for Mr. Right, if not nirvana or the answer to life's mysteries. Inevitably, I walked away with nothing and no one.

Despite the resulting pain, I was always searching outside myself for something or someone to make me happy, and I never felt a sense of inner peace. Life centered around my own desperate need for meaning, for healing, and for love.

I Didn't Have Enough Strength to Fool Myself

I can vividly recall one particularly hot day of that summer when I awoke under the pall of a lingering nightmare and with a sense of dread over life's insistence of a new day. I got up and stared at a frightening morning face in the bathroom mirror. Who was this person staring back at me? She had the same straight brown hair and brown eyes, but her complexion, normally an olive color, looked red and lumpy; and her features, normally youthful, drooped downward, forming a heavy depressive frown. Her eyes looked muddy, and her years looked advanced. When I tried to raise my eyebrows and facial muscles to feign happiness, she stared back at me forlorn and unconvinced. I wished I had never laid eyes on her.

I dragged myself to a nearby library to research something spiritually enlightening—or at least helpful. An urgent need to run to the bathroom interrupted my search and threw me into a frantic scurry. I lunged into a stall. Emergencies like this had become more frequent. I stood up to leave and looked down in horror to see the toilet bowl filled with blood. Lightheaded and stunned, and too scared to call a doctor, I walked out of the bathroom with a sick feeling, a mixture of dread and denial, swirling in the pit of my stomach.

Feeling like a stranger in my own body, I wandered down the aisles. Daunted by the stacks of books towering around me, I asked "The Universe" to guide me to the perfect book on life. I pulled books off the shelves, then put them back. I sat down confused and frozen in front of a computer catalogue system, then got up and walked off. I approached a librarian, then turned away silently. I sought knowledge, but exactly what kind I did not know. I wanted to check out a book that had all the answers to life's questions. But how could I look this up in a library catalogue system, much less ask a librarian to find it for me?

Defeated and lost, I sat down in a corner as a familiar wave of heavy, numbing, and vibrating tiredness glued me to the seat. My vision blurred as I stared out blankly at rows of books, under eyelids that wanted to clang shut with the weight of an iron gate. As I slumped in my seat, scared by my sudden fatigue and by rumbling feelings of panic and despair, I tried to meditate. I had heard that I was supposed to empty myself of all thoughts in order to dissipate into eternal nothingness, or eternal everything, I couldn't remember which. But my mind instead began fixating on a painful desire for a future husband.

Too tired for anything upright, I collapsed onto my side as a cavernous sadness began to swell within me. Fearing an oncoming flood of despair, I tried with a great force of will to dam my emotions, but I didn't have enough strength to fool myself. Tears began to streak sideways down my cheeks. To lift my hand to wipe them meant sacrificing the few drops of energy I felt I had left. So with my hands limp at my side, my limbs filling with cement, I let the tears fall, feeling dangerously wounded and alone. I stayed there for a couple of hours, as thoughts of my past years as a professional ballerina, full of energy and grace, flitted through my mind like a curse.

I was twenty-seven, and my health was declining rapidly, along with my sense of purpose and mental well-being. I began vomiting without cause, my hair was falling out more than usual, I was bleeding internally, and I couldn't tolerate most foods. I ached, my feet and back pulsated with pain, and without warning, energy continued to escape my deadened body as though life had dropped me. Worst of all, I felt sick inside my soul. At times, I would call out in guttural despair; at times, I would rage at life's inconveniences; and at times, I could not stop crying once I started.

"Can You Help Me? Can Anyone Help Me?"

In a last attempt at healing, I attended a Reiki hands-on "healing" workshop, and while I lay down on a massage table and the participants placed their hands on me, an energy poured into me that filled me with despair. I began to cry uncontrollably. Excusing myself, I climbed off the table before they were finished and curled up in a hidden corner to cry. My tears were gut-wrenching and yet provided no relief—only a lingering, eerie, fearful sadness.

When the workshop ended and people began to leave, I started to panic. I wanted to run up to someone, anyone nice, and shake the person and scream, "Can you help me? Can anyone help me?" Out of the corner of my eye, I saw a man walking away and almost ran up to him in the parking lot, but then I caught myself in my own madness and thought, "He can't help you. No human being can help you." Still sobbing, I got in my car and drove off, chanting the words, "Hold me. Hold me. Hold me!" and wondering if anyone on earth or beyond could hear me.

The only friend I had left that summer, the only person who could handle my extreme distress and crying spells, was a man named Joseph, who lived near my home on the West Coast. Time and again, Joseph patiently listened to me pour my sadness into the telephone receiver. I knew Joseph possessed something special, something that gave him deep contentment. While life tossed me about like a ship in raging seas, his rudder remained plunged deep into still waters. I couldn't hurt him with my pain. Talking to him, I felt safe. I knew he was different.

The morning after the Reiki workshop, as I lay in bed overcome by fatigue, I received a phone call that would change my life. It was Joseph. He told me that for the past six weeks he had been woken up in the middle of the night by a vision of me calling out to him saying, "Help me. Show me who you really are." He said he was confused by this, at first. Taking the message metaphorically, he began to help various women in his neighborhood—assisting young women with homework and walking elderly women across the street. But the more he disregarded the vision's request, the louder my image cried out, "Help me! Show me who you really are."

I had known Joseph for five years, and he had never talked to me about his faith, but that day on the phone, in his distinctive, soft, articulate voice, he began to speak to me about my soul and about God's love. His words pierced the inner recesses of my heart, and I started to feel light and expansive, as though my body were filling the entire room. "Christine," he said, "you are being saved."

We soon realized that God wanted me to see Joseph urgently. With the little energy I had left, I drummed up the courage to take a battery of medical tests, so many I can't now remember them. Then I flew to the West Coast for what was to be the most miraculous week of my life.

"Only Grace Has Saved You"

I looked forward to spending time in Joseph's room. Feeling so ill, I needed solace and rest. I had little strength of my own, and Joseph's room had always nurtured me. Joseph rented a room in Kensington, California, in a house so grand as to seem aloof. But his room felt like an oasis of peace—cozy, feminine, and inviting. Pictures of angels and Notre Dame Cathedral in France hung over wallpaper of Victorian ladies, their suitors, and distant sailboats. Beauty towered over function. Postcards and ribbons and trinkets were placed so delicately on display that whenever I bumped into one thing, about fifteen other things fell down at the same time. Two windows opened to an expanse of San Francisco Bay—to trees, sky, city lights, a Bay bridge, morning light, sunsets, and a backyard of short sculpted hedges, reminiscent of an ancient king's private garden. That week I would stare out those windows often.

The evening I arrived, I entered his home, placed my bag in a room adjacent to Joseph's (which he had reserved for me), placed myself on the bed without the energy to change clothes or lift up the covers, and went to sleep.

In the morning, Joseph woke up wondering how he might help me. "I'll need to pray today," he said, "and ask God why you're here. It would be good if you could spend the day in prayer as well."

"I don't know how to pray," I told him. "I've never prayed before."

Joseph looked at me incredulously, as though he'd encountered an extraterrestrial: "You mean to tell me you've never prayed?"

"Joseph! I wasn't raised with any religion! Just assume I have no clue."

Joseph grew introspective, looked at the ground, and began to shake his head. "I just can't imagine life without prayer," he said.

I slept most of the rest of the day, and when I woke up, Joseph had left a note saying that he had gone to the beach. Unsure of what to do with myself, I decided to take a twilight walk around the block. As soon as I walked out the door, I felt a happiness and tranquility that seemed otherworldly. My emotional torment and my normal body aches, foot pain, and fatigue had left me. As I walked along the neighborhood sidewalks, my feet felt like they hovered slightly above ground; my legs lifted and lowered weightlessly, as though I were walking on the moon; and my eyes could see a supernatural beauty in nature that I had never been able to see before nor ever since. Flowers, shrubs, and trees seemed illuminated from within. As I looked around me, I blinked several times to test if what I was seeing was real. It was, and I began to cry in wonder.

After an hour had passed, I walked back to Joseph's home. As I waited for him to return, the gift of expansive peace slowly subsided, and I again felt restricted to my aching body, yet not the same. While my physical symptoms had crept back, my spirit remained joyful. When Joseph finally arrived, I told him about my heavenly walk. His pensive reaction puzzled me. Normally, he openly delighted in the good fortune of others, but as I spoke, he listened to me quietly and was slow to respond. "How was your time at the beach?" I asked.

Joseph sat down in a chair next to me, stared into the space in front of him, and said nothing.

Wondering if he had heard me, I asked again, "How was your time at the beach?"

I noticed that that his upper lip was trembling. Sighing deeply, he began to speak.

He told me that as he was sitting on the sand, he suddenly felt spiritually attacked. A weight of evil pressed down upon him from above, and he felt like his bones were literally being crushed. Fearing that he might not survive under the weight, he called out to God and to Mary for help, and finally the assault grew weaker and eventually stopped. He then looked up to see the outline of a dark demonic figure, glaring at him and screeching a hideous cry of angry defeat as it skimmed along the ocean, moving further and further away, until it fell away from view.

Bewildered, he looked down at the sand around him and couldn't believe his eyes. It was covered with his blood. Then he noticed that so, too, were areas of his skin. He had sweated blood from the stress of battling Satan. What he had experienced in the spiritual realm had affected him physically. Joseph peered behind himself to see a couple strolling by on the beach who, when they noticed him, looked fearful and began to walk faster. "I'd better wash myself in the sea," he thought. "Lord knows what I look like."

"I didn't know until now," Joseph said to me in a serious tone, "that the devil doesn't just live inside human beings, but is actually a being—conscious, fully alive, and deadly."

Not knowing what to say, I stammered in a whisper, "It's incredible that as I was experiencing a moment of freedom from all my torment for the first time, you were being tormented like never before."

"It's not a coincidence, Christine."

"What do you mean?"

"All the demons that were in you came after me."

"Oh, my God. What?! Why?"

"They knew I was going to lead you to God, and they were furious."

"How many were in me?"

"You were a way station."

I recoiled at the thought of what had lived inside of me. I started to feel sick, horrified that I was part of what happened to Joseph.

"Christine," he said. "What have you been involved in that caused all this?"

I honestly didn't know. At Joseph's request, I began to tell him things about my life that I had kept secret: my depression after having to quit ballet; my intimate relationships with a string of boyfriends; my brief affairs, two of which were with married men I had worked with at a restaurant; my New Age retreats and practices. Joseph grew pale and looked increasingly dismayed as I continued. He told me that premarital sex was wrong, that God never wanted me to be thrown around from heartbreak to heartbreak, that sexual behavior put me at risk for getting deadly viruses, and that if I was going to unite with a man and become one with him, God would want that man to commit to me with a vow in marriage and love me for life. Then sex could be safe for my soul.

"The Church doesn't just make this stuff up, you know," he said. "You lost God's protection when you lost your virginity, and you opened yourself up to the demonic realm. With every person you slept with, more demons entered your soul. And you also hurt the souls of those you were with."

I defended myself, saying that no one ever told me that premarital sex was wrong. How was I to know? Then I remembered how, at a deep level inside myself, I did know something felt wrong, but I had ignored the feeling. I couldn't bring myself to defend my participation in adultery, though. I had rationalized away any feelings of conscience at the time, saying to myself, "He must not have a very good marriage, anyway. If it's already bad, I'm not causing any more harm." But I never forgot the evening when I served my lover's wife at a restaurant table. She looked up to thank me with sweet eyes and an innocent smile that pierced my conscience like a fiery lance. My whole body flushed with a warm rush of shame.

Struggling to find something redemptive about my life, I said to Joseph, "Well, at least I was growing in my spirituality by going to New Age workshops and working toward a higher consciousness."

"Christine, none of that helped you. The New Age movement does not honor the true God. Many New Age practices break God's first commandment, which says, 'I am the Lord your God; you shall not have strange gods before me.' Time and time again, God reached out to you to help you change your path, but you walked right up to the edge of a precipice and were about to fall off. Only grace has saved you."

I sat in stunned silence and put my head in my hands, barely able to breathe, devastated by the news that my search for love and meaning was not only a waste of my life, but the destruction of it.

That night, I lowered myself to my knees and cried. Exhausted by the truth and by sickness, I dropped my head to the floor and, one by one, remembered each man I had been with. I told God I was sorry for what I had done. Then I lifted up to God my whole history of spiritual confusion and said, "I'm sorry that I've offended you. I'm sorry that I hurt you so much. Please forgive me."

You Are as Blessed as You Are Loved

I slept that night as though in a tomb. My health had declined to a perilous degree. I wanted help. I wanted God. But I wanted nothing to do with Jesus or Mary. For years I had wanted nothing to do with them.

Once when I had seen a picture of the Madonna and Child, it made me so angry that I wanted it taken down. Another time, I had read a self-help book that I had enjoyed except for its fleeting references to Jesus. I knew that Jesus and Mary were fanciful figures for the hopeless and misguided. For me, their names and images had provoked ire. I had always disliked them intensely.

But Jesus decided to save me, a sinner. I will never know why he chose me, and I do not have the words to express my gratitude. I would not be alive were it not for divine grace, unmerited and unasked for.

Three days after my arrival on the West Coast, as I lay down in Joseph's room with my eyes closed and half-asleep, I felt the presence of God within and around me. In my mind's eye, I saw a gray, pulsating mass. A few seconds later, I heard a loud "pop" sound inside of me, and the mass disappeared. Then I opened my eyes to see Joseph sitting next to me. "Did you hear that?" I asked him.

"No. What did you hear?" he asked.

I explained what had just happened. He paused pensively and said, "It was important that you came here as soon as you did."

"Why?"

"Christine. Jesus just cured you of cancer."

"What?!" I exclaimed, catching my breath. "What are you saying?"

"You had cancer, and you had six weeks to live."

"What!? How do you know that?"

"I was deep in prayer just now, and Mary came to me. She spoke to me. At the same time you were sensing the presence of God with you, Mary was telling me that she saw you flailing in life, like a fish that couldn't find water, even though an ocean was always just next to you. She took pity on you and asked her Son to save you."

I sat upright, speechless. I tried to say a word, but couldn't. Somehow, I knew he had spoken the truth.

Over the next three days, nearly all my physical symptoms vanished, and over time my energy returned. I called the East Coast to find out that a pap smear I had received was abnormal, and I was told I had to come in to see a doctor immediately; but feeling completely assured and at peace, I didn't worry and didn't follow up on it. I've had healthy checkups ever since, and I've learned that promiscuity can lead to cervical cancer through exposure to the human papilloma virus.

My sexual sins had helped bring about both the death of my soul and the death of my body. But Jesus, at Mary's request, had saved my soul and my life. Even though I had hated them, they had always loved me.

Heaven Was Rejoicing Because One Sinner Had Been Saved

The next day, Mary again spoke to Joseph and told him that I should pray the rosary whenever I needed her help, and she would come to me. Jesus also told him that I should sin no more, join the Catholic Church, and help bring to it "compassion, love, kindness, and generosity." I had never before set foot in a Catholic Church as anything but a tourist, but I wanted to learn how I could "sign up."

"If you had died before Jesus saved you," Joseph told me, "you would have been in excruciating pain, not only in your body, because the cancer would have spread to your bones, but also in your soul, because you would have wasted much of your life. Then after death, you would have entered into a place of suffering and remorse for what would have seemed like thousands of years."

"Thousands of years?" I asked him in disbelief. "You got that in prayer, too?"

"Yes," he said. "Time is different in purgatory than here. To you, it would have seemed like an eternity before you could enter heaven."

I told him I thought I was going to be born again into a different body here on earth after I died, but he assured me that that belief wasn't true. "We are born into this life only once," he explained, "and where we end up—whether in heaven, purgatory, or hell—depends on how we live our lives here.

"Heaven," he said, "is worth anything—any suffering on earth. Souls experience a joy there that is indescribable. They are completely fulfilled, and they live amidst beauty that doesn't exist here on earth."

"You've actually experienced heaven?" I asked him.

He blushed and looked away, then grew silent and contemplative and didn't answer. After a few moments, he turned his face toward me, caught my eyes with his, and said, "Even if a person's sins are scarlet, heartfelt repentance can lead one into paradise."

The evening after I was cured, I heard a symphony—a soft, lilting piece of music I had never heard before. I was in Joseph's room and thought that perhaps the radio was on. I checked everywhere—in the hall, out the window, under the bed, even in his desk drawers, to see where the music might be playing; but I soon realized that the beautiful music was coming from within me. I realized then that heaven was rejoicing because one sinner had been saved, and the heavenly hosts were letting me join in the celebration.

That same night, Joseph had a dream. He saw me staring with amazement at my own hand to see it brilliant with radiant light. I gasped as my eyes traveled from my hand to the rest of my body. Divine light was permeating and illuminating all of me. "See Christine," he said, "you walk in light. You worry about the pain in your feet and your body, yet this is who you are. You are as blessed as you are loved. You are a feather on the breath of God."

God Had Recreated Me

My days with Joseph surpassed my own understanding, and although my life continued to be scattered with small miracles, nothing compared with the intense outpouring of supernatural grace that brought me back to life. Through Joseph, Jesus showered me with more piercing love, genuine truth, and immediate attention than I had been able to receive in all my previous years. Jesus entered into my life's desert wasteland, scorched and starved, and he breathed his Spirit into mine. Green sprouts of hope and small yellow flowers of joy peered out of my heart and budded through the cracks. I sat in church every day, crying and crying out of gratitude. In one week, God had recreated me.

Before Jesus healed me, I could not give myself to others. Whenever I did, a pit of desperate need always pulled me back into selfishness. I could not find meaning. Life was a series of random disappointing events. But after my conversion, God gave me a purpose: to love him above all things and to love my neighbor as myself. Finally, I could look at the world and wonder what I could give, not just what I could get.

In the years that followed, I learned what it meant to be Christian. I prepared for and received the sacrament of baptism, a gift from above of unmeasured grace through which Christ gave me a share in his divine life. I worked for three years toward a master's degree in theological studies at the Jesuit School of Theology at Berkeley, where all the great mysteries of life were at my fingertips, like ripe blackberries ready to be plucked. My last summer there, I enjoyed learning how to be a spiritual director. Then I studied for two years at the University of California at Berkeley and received a master's degree in social welfare, through which I learned the practicalities of living my faith on behalf of those in need.

I ministered to women in prison, people with AIDS, and as resident minister in a college dorm. Then I began working as a social worker and bereavement counselor with the dying and grieving through hospice care, which prepared me for a later job as a post-abortion counselor and education director with a license in clinical social work. In addition, I worked as a spiritual director, inspirational speaker, retreat leader, and parish mission preacher. And by God's grace, I entered into the sacrament of marriage with a loving man named John.

I Respected Mary, But I Could Not Feel Her

At this point in my story, God took me on a healing journey to meet someone I had summarily disregarded. She had looked down from heaven, taken pity on me, and asked her Son to save me. She had invited me to pray the rosary, which I ignored. She had revealed herself as my constant support, but I never called upon her. I respected her as an awesome, powerful presence,

Queen of heaven and earth, the Immaculate Conception, free from sin, overseeing all her children with endearing love; but I, myself, could not feel her. For me, Mary remained a distant figure, frozen inside the contours of her statues. This sense of separation continued, even as I became intrigued by her apparitions in a small town called Medjugorje in Bosnia and Herzegovina, on the other side of the world.

When I learned that Mary had come to earth with five primary requests, I reminded myself that this was the same Mary who had helped save my life, so the least I could do was answer her call. She was asking for frequent reception of the eucharist, Bible reading, prayer—especially the rosary, monthly confession, and fasting on bread and water on Wednesdays and Fridays. Easier thought than done. I limped through her messages: I began to pray the rosary sporadically, at best; I rarely read the Bible because I figured I had studied enough of it in theology school; I went to confession whenever I felt like it; and my first attempt at fasting gave me a pounding headache, so I ate ice cream instead.

It wasn't until I sensed a calling in my heart to take my husband, John, to Medjugorje that I received the grace to live Mary's messages in earnest. Just four months after our marriage, we boarded a plane for a week-long pilgrimage in this little, unassuming town across the world.

I Felt United with Heaven

Medjugorje captivated us. We didn't know that a physical place on earth could contain so much of heaven. Never before Medjugorje had we experienced such intense spiritual communion, such palpable belief, everywhere we looked. In the dead of winter, the town church, St. James, overflowed with people every evening. And those unable to enter stood outside in the cold just to hear the words of the rosary and the Mass echo through the town from a loudspeaker. We immersed ourselves in the fervent liturgies and in the faithful crowd, kneeling humbly in prayer, ardently singing the beautiful local songs during adoration of the Blessed Sacrament. We marveled at the long, long lines of people waiting for their turn to confess; the miracles; the converting hearts; and the nightly climbing of Apparition Hill, with people marching slowly on the rocky path, guided by the moonlight, saying the rosary together aloud, until they arrived on the spot where Mary first appeared to the visionaries.

Surrounded by the sound of prayer, the smell of fresh air, the sight of reverence and bright faces, I often felt out of this world. I felt united with heaven and could feel the presence of God. Worrying was impossible. When I tried, I couldn't. The power of belief in God was so strong in Medjugorje that it could almost be touched. Yet still, in that place of extraordinary grace, when my mind filled with thoughts of my mother in heaven, an odd indifference came over my heart. "Please, Mom," I asked her. "Help me to feel you."

Mary Never Gave Up on Me

Months after my return home, I was scheduled to have an ablation—a medical procedure to correct my rapid heartbeats. The procedure involved inserting two long wires with electrodes into upper arteries of my leg, and funneling them all the way up into my heart. I felt frightened, and although the procedure went well, the recovery was painful, and I craved support from friends and family—especially, for some reason, from my mother. But my mother didn't call. I felt so disregarded and in need of motherly love that I began to weep. My pain ripped open old wounds that overwhelmed me, so I called a friend for support, and in the midst of our conversation, she exclaimed, "Oh! I sense Mary. She's here, she's here!—I feel her presence so strongly. She's waited for this moment all your life. She's been there for you ever since you were a little girl. She wants you to let her into your heart, and she's telling me that now you're finally able to feel her."

I could barely speak. I allowed her words to wash over me gently, like a lullaby soothing the plaintive cries of an infant. For the first time, I let Mary's love heal my pain. For the first time, I could feel my Mother in heaven. As her light, comforting presence wrapped itself tenderly around me, she somehow entered the open cracks in my heart, and the cold chasm I had long felt between us vanished.

As I look back, it is hard for me to understand why Mary never gave up on me, waiting years for me to accept her embrace. And I will never fully grasp why she asked her Son to save me. What kind of love waits so patiently, never losing its fervor, even in the face of anger, unbelief, and indifference?

The complete love of a mother.

Dear children, this is the reason for my presence among you for such a long time: to lead you to Jesus. I want to save you and, through you, to save the whole world.

Many people now live without faith; some don't even want to hear about Jesus, and yet they still want peace and fulfillment! Children, this is the reason why I need your prayer: Prayer is the only way to save the human race.

—Mary's message of July 30, 1987, from *Medjugorje Day by Day*

FOR PRAYERFUL REFLECTION

The heart of the woman with the alabaster jar in Luke 7, who kissed Jesus' feet and bathed them with her tears, is reflected in the heart of Christine, who two thousand years later sat in church every day, weeping with gratitude, overcome by the magnitude of what Jesus had done for her.

> A Pharisee invited [Jesus] to dine with him, and he entered the Pharisee's house and reclined at table. Now there was a sinful woman in the city who learned that he was at table in the house of the Pharisee. Bringing an alabaster flask of ointment, she stood behind him at his feet weeping and began to bathe his feet with her tears. Then she wiped them with her hair, kissed them, and anointed them with the ointment.
>
> When the Pharisee who had invited him saw this he said to himself, "If this man were a prophet, he would know who and what sort of woman this is who is touching him, that she is a sinner."
>
> Then [Jesus] turned to the woman and said to Simon, "Do you see this woman? When I entered your house, you did not give me water for my feet, but she has bathed them with her tears and wiped them with her hair.
>
> "You did not give me a kiss, but she has not ceased kissing my feet since the time I entered. You did not anoint my head with oil, but she anointed my feet with ointment. So I tell you, her many sins have been forgiven; hence, she has shown great love. But the one to whom little is forgiven, loves little."
>
> He said to her, "Your sins are forgiven."
>
> The others at table said to themselves, "Who is this who even forgives sins?"
>
> But he said to the woman, "Your faith has saved you; go in peace."
>
> —Luke 7:36–50

1. We are not told what occurred prior to this scripture scene. Clearly something transformative happened to the woman with the alabaster jar even before she burst in the door. Jesus must have touched her so deeply that she, a known sinner, entered the house of a Pharisee just to give thanks to the One who loved her into a new existence. Is there a moment or a time you can remember when God reached into your life in an indelible way? What happened? What was your response?

2. For much of her life, Christine didn't know how to pray. Her friend Joseph was startled by this because he couldn't imagine life without prayer. In her messages from Medjugorje, Mary's most repeated request is that we pray. In her message of September 25, 1987, she says:

> Dear children! Today also I want to call you all to prayer. Let prayer be your life. Dear children, dedicate your time only to Jesus, and He will give you everything that you are seeking. He will reveal Himself to you in fullness. . . .

How important is prayer to you? What tends to distract you from prayer? What may lead you to believe you don't have time for it? What we do with our time often reveals the priorities in our hearts. Where is prayer on your daily list of activities?

3. In times of suffering, do you find yourself moving closer to God or further away from him? Consider whether there are certain sufferings or problems that you feel comfortable approaching God with and others that you don't. Why? What's the difference? Do you remember him when things are going well? How might you stay close to God through both joys and sufferings, trials and triumphs?

4. Christine experimented with various New Age activities, unaware that God forbids such activities because they tend toward the occult—mixing the truth with lies—while pointing us away from his Son and his Church. In her effort to heal her pain and confusion,

she tried tarot card readings, psychics, and many other things. In your search for knowledge or comfort, have you dabbled in what could be considered the realm of the occult? Have you ever done something that you thought at the time was okay only to realize later that it wasn't what God had in mind for you? If so, you can ask God to heal and cleanse you from the effects of these activities, particularly by mentioning them in the sacrament of reconciliation. There Jesus reaches gently within our souls, fulfilling our deepest yearnings for healing, meaning, acceptance, and love.

5. Christine sought comfort in intimate relationships, only to find herself increasingly wounded and lost. Pope John Paul II asked men and women to reflect honestly on their experience of sexuality, offering the poignant question, "Have you found lasting peace and joy in using sexual intimacy outside of God's original design?" Ponder this question in light of your own experiences or that of someone you know.

6. Jesus desires to lead all of us into a life of holiness and joy, and one day, to our heavenly home, where there is no more suffering and there are no more tears. To help us, he has sent his Mother to earth. Her requests come straight from God's heart, with great love and great seriousness. As scripture and the history of Marian apparitions have taught us, unwanted consequences befall us when we don't heed God's call. Mary goes as far to say in her message above that "prayer is the only way to save the human race." Mary's primary requests are that we pray daily (especially the rosary), receive the eucharist often, read our Bible, go to confession once a month, and fast on bread and water on Wednesdays and Fridays. With gentle pleading, she is asking this of all of us. Will you heed her call?

FAITH EXERCISE

Anyone who has lived without God knows that life can seem like a meaningless string of events, imbued with an existential angst that begs the question, "What is the point of my life?" Anyone who has embarked upon a journey toward God also knows that the trail, once found, can seem treacherous at times, with blind spots and unexpected turns. And yet Jesus is there for all of us, inviting us to believe and to allow him to eradicate fear from our lives at every step as he replaces it with trust and love. In what areas of your life would you like him to give you more trust in his providential care? In what areas of your life would you like him to give you more love? Ask him now for what you wish. He longs to grant your request.

Dear children! I am calling you because I need you. I need hearts ready for immeasurable love—hearts that are not burdened by vanity—hearts that are ready to love as my Son loved—that are ready to sacrifice themselves as my Son sacrificed himself. I need you. In order to come with me, forgive yourselves, forgive others and adore my Son. Adore him also for those who have not come to know him, those who do not love him. Therefore, I need you; therefore, I call you. Thank you.

— Mary's message of July 2, 2009

APPENDIX

A Brief Account of the Medjugorje Apparitions

On June 24, 1981, in a remote village in the former communist Yugoslavia, two teenage girls, Mirjana and Ivanka, went for a walk. As they exchanged the latest news in their lives, Ivanka suddenly noticed a light high up on Mount Podbrdo, the large hill behind the village. Looking up, she saw a woman, radiating with light, hovering above the ground on a cloud and holding a baby in her arms. Ivanka said to Mirjana, "I think that Our Lady is on the hill." Mirjana, not bothering to glance up, responded glibly, "Yes, Our Lady has nothing better to do than to come to the two of us."

Brushing off Ivanka's strange behavior, she left and walked back toward the village, but she soon felt a great urge to return. When she did, she found Ivanka in the same spot, still staring at the hill, mesmerized. "Look at it now, please," said Ivanka. Mirjana looked up and saw a beautiful woman with blue eyes and long, dark hair, dressed in a gray dress and a white veil, with a baby in her arms and a crown of twelve stars around her head. Mirjana says of that instant, "All the possible emotions that exist I felt in my heart at the same time. To put it simply, I was not aware if I was alive or dead."

Just then, a friend of theirs named Vicka was passing by, looking for the two of them, and when she, too, saw the woman on the hill, she jumped out of her slippers and ran headlong back to the village. A few moments later, a teenage boy named

Ivan walked by on his way home carrying apples in his arms, and upon seeing the woman, threw down the apples and ran away. Then Mirjana said to Ivanka, "Who knows what's going on? It's better for us to go home as well."

The next day, all four children felt drawn back to the same spot (which is now called Apparition Hill). Vicka ran to get her friend, Marija, and ten-year-old Jakov, and all six children saw the beautiful woman. Then again the following day, July 26, they saw her—this time with nearly the entire village present. On that day, more than five thousand people saw the visionaries bathed in an immense light and believed.

As soon as the woman appeared, Vicka, at her grandmother's urging, sprinkled holy water on her in the sign of the cross and said, "If you are Satan, go away from us." The woman just smiled with an expression of immense love, and then she spoke:

> Do not be afraid, dear angels.
> I am the Mother of God.
> I am the Queen of Peace.
> I am the mother of all people.[1]

Thus began Mary's daily apparitions to the six children, the longest-occurring series of apparitions in Church history. They continue to this day. Why has she been appearing so long? She answers this question in her message of January 25, 2009:

> . . . I am with you for this long because you are on the wrong path. Only with my help, little children, you will open your eyes. There are many of those who, by living my messages, comprehend that they are on the way of holiness towards eternity. . . .[2]

On the second day of the Medjugorje apparitions, Marija saw Mary crying and carrying a wooden cross. "Peace, peace, peace!" were the words she spoke. "Be reconciled! Only peace!"[3] Twenty-eight years later, in her message of April 25, 2009, she calls out to us again:

> Dear children! Today I call you all to pray for peace and to witness it in your families so that peace may become the highest treasure on this peaceless earth. I am your Queen of Peace and your mother. I desire to lead you on the way of peace, which comes only from God. Therefore, pray, pray, pray. Thank you for having responded to my call.[4]

Mary is appearing to a world intent on destroying itself in order to urge her children to return to the ways of God. To show to the world that her presence and words are true and real, Our Lady has promised that when she stops appearing, a visible and lasting sign, undeniably of God, will be left on the spot of her first apparition.

Mary has chosen to appear in Medjugorje and to give the world messages in order to continue the work she set out to do when she appeared to three young children in Fatima, Portugal, in 1917. Part of her message from August 25, 1991, states:

> . . . I call all of you, dear children, to pray and fast still more firmly . . . so that, with your help, everything I desire to realize through the secrets I began in Fatima, may be fulfilled. I call you, dear children, to grasp the importance of my coming and the seriousness of the situation. . . .[5]

In the Church-approved apparitions at Fatima, Mary gave the three young seers three secrets; in an earlier approved apparition in La Salette, France, in 1846, she gave two young seers two secrets. These have all since been revealed. The Blessed Mother is now in the process of giving ten secrets to each of the six visionaries in Medjugorje, some of whom have received all ten. The secrets will be revealed in the not-too-distant future, as the visionary Mirjana has been asked by Mary to help publicize them through a priest at the appointed time. Mary and the visionaries tell us, however, not to focus on the secrets; only to focus on our own personal conversion, here and now.

Strongly urging everyone to "pray, pray, pray," Mary has given five specific means to holiness that she wishes of us, in order to truly live her messages: frequent attendance of the Holy Mass, monthly confession, Bible reading, daily prayer (especially the rosary), and fasting on bread and water on Wednesdays and Fridays—all done with the heart. "I am not God," she said in her message in December 1983, "I need your prayers and sacrifices to help me."[6] And "you have forgotten that with prayer and fasting you can ward off wars, suspend natural laws."[7]

In many of Mary's messages, she encourages us to live in joy. On June 6, 1986, she said:

> Dear children, these days the Lord is allowing me to intercede for more graces for you. Thus I urge you once more to pray, dear children. Pray without ceasing. That way I can give you the joy which the Lord has given me. With these graces, dear children, your sufferings can be turned to joy. I am your mother and I want to help you.[8]

Since the apparitions began, the visionaries, who humbly say that they are not important and no more holy than you or me, spend as many as six hours or more daily in prayer and fast on bread and water up to three times a week. Following their initial fright, the six young visionaries quickly lost their fear of the Virgin Mary. They say her love for them and all of humanity cannot be expressed in words, and that to be in her presence is like being in heaven. They speak of her as "beautiful beyond anything in this world."[9] In the early days of the apparitions, they once asked her, "Why are you so beautiful?" and she responded, "I am beautiful because I love. You, too, are beautiful when you love."[10]

Pope John Paul II made several personal statements giving his wholehearted support of the apparitions. "If I weren't the Pope," he said, "I'd be in Medjugorje already!" as reported April 29, 1989, by Bishop Paul Hnilica, S.J., Auxiliary Bishop of Rome, after having been admonished by the Holy Father for not stopping in Medjugorje on his return trip to Rome.

To Monsignor Maurillo Kreiger, former bishop of Florianopolis in Brazil, the pope said, "Medjugorje, Medjugorje, it's the spiritual heart of the world."[11] When the visionary Mirjana traveled to Rome, Pope John Paul II learned that she was there and asked to see her in person in the nearby town of Castle Grandolfo at his summer residence. There he expressed similar sentiments to her. "I know everything about Medjugorje," He said. "I've been following Medjugorje. Ask pilgrims to pray for my intentions, to keep, to take good care of Medjugorje, because Medjugorje is hope for the entire world. And if I were not Pope, I would have been in Medjugorje a long time ago."[12]

Since 1981, when the apparitions to the children began, more than 45 million pilgrims from all over the world have been to Medjugorje, including the 180 bishops, forty-two archbishops, eight cardinals, and many thousands of priests who have publicly visited Medjugorje.[13] This does not include all of the clerics who have chosen to go privately for their own personal pilgrimage.[14] Each day, villagers and pilgrims pray for hours in the local church, while others wait in the long lines for confession. All day, and often into the night, pilgrims climb Apparition Hill, where Mary first appeared to the children, lending their prayers to the sacred atmosphere. Nearby, pilgrims also climb Cross Mountain, upon which the villagers erected by hand a fifteen-ton, thirty-six-foot-high cross in 1933 to commemorate the 1900th anniversary of the crucifixion. Mary told the children that she chose to appear in Medjugorje because of the strong faith she found in the village, and she continues to call people from across the globe to make a pilgrimage there to encounter her Son in a special way. Those who heed her call with an open spirit find themselves in a place of extraordinary peace, where rosaries turn gold, the sun dances and spins in the sky, and miracles, conversions, and healings abound—most importantly, the healing of the human heart.

Notes

1. Story compiled from Janice Connell's *The Visions of the Children* (New York: St. Martin's Griffin, 1997), 10; *Medjugorje Magazine*, May 2002 Special issue, 14; and a videotape of Mirjana telling her story to pilgrims in December 2001, provided by Fiat Voluntas Tua.

2. www.medjugorje.org/msg09.htm.

3. Richard Beyer, *Medjugorje Day by Day* (Notre Dame, IN: Ave Maria Press, 1993), 6.

4. www.medjugorje.org/msg09.htm.

5. Mary's message of August 25, 1991, from Sister Emmanuel, *Medjugorje, the '90s* (Santa Barbara, CA: Queenship Publishing Co., 1997), 69.

6. Beyer, *Medjugorje Day by Day,* July 14 meditation.

7. Wayne Weible, *Medjugorje the Message* (Brewster, MA: Paraclete Press, 1989), 44.

8. Beyer, *Medjugorje Day by Day,* July 27 meditation.

9. Ibid., 5.

10. Mirjana's story as told by her, captured on videotape to pilgrims in December 2001, provided by Fiat Voluntas Tua.

11. www.medjugorje.org/pope.htm. For more authenticated quotes from Pope John Paul II, see *Medjugorje and the Church* by Denis Nolan.

12. www.spiritofmedjugorje.org/june2009.htm.

13. Miravalle and Weible, *Are the Medjugorje Apparitions Authentic?* back cover.

14. Denis Nolan, *Medjugorje and the Church*, 4th edition (Goleta, CA: Queenship Publishing, 2007), 36–45.

Resources

Medjugorje

For information on pilgrimages to Medjugorje, hosted by visionary Mirjana Dragicevic-Soldo, contact:

Trinity Pilgrimages
Jim Benzow, Managing Director
8742 E. Via Taz Norte
Scottsdale, AZ 85258
(480) 443-3912 or (602) 319-5289
trinitypilgrimage@cox.net
www.trinitypilgrimage.com

Recommended reading:

Beyer, Richard J. *Medjugorje Day by Day*. Notre Dame, IN: Ave Maria Press, 1993.

Connell, Janice. *The Visions of the Children*. New York: St. Martin's Griffin, 1997.

———. *Queen of the Cosmos*. Brewster, MA: Paraclete Press, 1990.

Faricy, Robert, and Lucy Rooney. *A Medjugorje Retreat*. New York: Alba House, 1989.

Weible, Wayne. *Medjugorje the Message*. Brewster, MA: Paraclete Press, 1989.

———. *Final Harvest*. Oak Lawn, IL: CMJ Marian Publishers, 2002.

Miravalle, Mark, Dr., and Wayne Weible. *Are the Medjugorje Apparitions Authentic?* Hiawassee, GA: New Hope Press, 2008.

Nolan, Denis. *Medjugorje and the Church*, 4th edition. Goleta, CA: Queenship Publishing, 2007.

Medjugorje Magazine

Larry Eck and Mary Sue Eck, editors
P.O. Box 373
Westmont, IL 60559-0373
For subscriptions call (630) 968-5268
www.medjugormag.com

A list of websites dedicated to Medjugorje:
www.medjugorjepilgrim.com/Links.html

To receive Mary's monthly messages via e-mail,
contact sshawl@medjweb.com

Foundation for the Children of the Andes

As of 2008, fifty-five thousand children have come through the Foundation for the Children of the Andes, where they received an education, love, tenderness, a church in which to pray, and a future. Once they had no hope and no one to care for them, but now they are doctors and engineers, lawyers, and most importantly, they themselves are now helping their families and other children.

Should you wish to make a donation to the Foundation for the Children of the Andes, please make checks out to "Children of the Sewers" and mail them to:

Children of the Sewers
Weible Columns Inc.
P.O. Box 10
Hiawassee, GA 30546
(706) 896-6061

When you make a donation, you will be sent a tax-deductible receipt in the mail. For details, e-mail weiblecols@windstream.net.

Post-Abortion Healing

Rachel's Vineyard Ministries holds weekend retreats for healing after abortion. For information, visit www.rachelsvineyard.org, or call their toll-free confidential number: (877) HOPE-4-ME [467-3463].

Project Rachel is a Catholic network of professional counselors and priests trained to provide one-on-one spiritual and psychological care for those who are suffering because of an abortion. You can visit their website at www.hopeafterabortion.com.

Natural Family Planning (NFP)

For educational resources concerning the harms of contraception visit www.onemoresoul.com.

Natural Family Planning (NFP) is natural birth control without the use of artificial pills or invasive procedures. NFP's effectiveness in avoiding pregnancy is equal to or better than drugs or devices on the market. Familiarity with an NFP method also increases a woman's chance of pregnancy when she is trying to have a child. For information and instruction, visit the following websites:

The Creighton Model "FertilityCare System"
www.creightonmodel.com

Billings Ovulation Method of Natural Fertility Regulation
www.billings-centre.ab.ca

The Sympto-Thermal Method taught by the Couple
to Couple League
www.ccli.org

The Cenacolo Community

In the United States:
Our Lady of Hope Community
24 Cathedral Place Suite 307
St. Augustine, FL 32084
www.comunitacenacolo.org

In Medjugorje and throughout the world:
www.hopereborn.org

The New Age Movement

Recommended reading:

Information about corruption and abuse in Siddha Yoga:
www.LeavingSiddhaYoga.net

An extensive list of articles:
Go to www.LeavingSiddhaYoga.net/frames2.htm, click on
"articles," scroll down to O Guru, Guru, Guru, by Lis Har-
ris, *The New Yorker*, November 14, 1994, an important pub-
lished piece that explains the problems of Siddha Yoga.

Groothuis, Douglas. *Unmasking the New Age*. Downers
Grove, IL: Intervarsity Press, 1986.

———. *Confronting the New Age*. Downers Grove, IL: Intervarsity Press, 1988.

Michaelsen, Johanna. *The Beautiful Side of Evil*. Eugene, OR:
Harvest House Publishers, 1982.

Pacwa, S.J., Mitch. *Catholics and the New Age*. Ann Arbor,
MI: Servant Publications, 1992.

Videotape

On the Edge of His Grace includes a brief interview with John Watkins (chapter 2) and is available through:

Focus Worldwide Network
229 North Vermont Street
Covington, LA 70433

To order call (985) 635-0333. Video is order number F-872.

NEED AN INSPIRATIONAL SPEAKER?

E-mail holychoices@gmail.com to book Christine Watkins (chapter 6), John Watkins (chapter 2), and/or Michael Crotty (chapter 5) for your next Catholic event.

LEARN MORE. . .

For further information on Christine Watkins's retreat, "Making Holy Choices: Discerning God's Will in Your Life," please go to www.holychoices.org. And to learn more about her parish mission, "Faith Alive," please visit www.enliveningfaith.org.

MARY AND MEDJUGORJE RESOURCES

You can also visit www.medjugorjemiracles.com to read about Mary and Medjugorje, listen to moving testimonies, see videos and pictures of miracles, pray with Mary through weekly postings of her messages with commentaries, and post your own Medjugorje stories for others to see.

Christine Watkins holds a Master of Theological Studies degree from the Jesuit School of Theology at Berkeley and a Master of Social Welfare degree from the University of California at Berkeley's School of Social Welfare. She is trained in Ignatian spirituality and discernment, with ten years of work experience as a spiritual director, bereavement counselor, inspirational speaker, and retreat leader. Watkins currently lives in California with her husband and sons. Visit her online at www.christinewatkins.com.

Founded in 1865, Ave Maria Press,
a ministry of the Congregation of
Holy Cross, is a Catholic publishing
company that serves the spiritual and
formative needs of the Church and its
schools, institutions, and ministers;
Christian individuals and families; and
others seeking spiritual nourishment.

For a complete listing of titles from

Ave Maria Press

Sorin Books

Forest of Peace

Christian Classics

visit www.avemariapress.com

 ave maria press / Notre Dame, IN 46556
A Ministry of the Indiana Province of Holy Cross